Core Connections, Course 2
Foundations for Algebra Toolkit

Managing Editors / Authors

Leslie Dietiker, Ph.D., Director of Curriculum (Both Editions)
Boston University
Boston, MA

Evra Baldinger (First Edition)
University of California, Berkeley
Berkeley, CA

Barbara Shreve (First Edition)
San Lorenzo High School
San Lorenzo, CA

Michael Kassarjian (Second Edition)
CPM Educational Program
Kensington, CA

Misty Nikula (Second Edition)
CPM Educational Program
Bellingham, WA

Technical Assistants: Toolkit

Hannah Coyner
Sacramento, CA

Sarah Maile
Sacramento, CA

Cover Art

Jonathan Weast
Sacramento, CA

Program Directors

Leslie Dietiker, Ph.D.
Boston University
Boston, MA

Lori Hamada
CPM Educational Program
Fresno, CA

Brian Hoey
CPM Educational Program
Sacramento, CA

Judy Kysh, Ph.D.
Departments of Education and Mathematics
San Francisco State University, CA

Tom Sallee, Ph.D.
Department of Mathematics
University of California, Davis

5 6 7 8 9   20 19 18 17 16

Printed in the United States of America   ISBN: 978-1-60328-095-2

Core Connections: Foundations for Algebra Course 2 Toolkit

Dear Math Student,

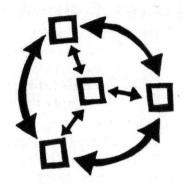

Welcome to your *Core Connections: Foundations for Algebra* Toolkit! It is designed to help you as you learn math throughout the school year. Inside, you will find all of the Math Notes from your textbook that have useful information about the topics you will study. You will also be able to write in your Toolkit so that you can keep track of what you have learned in your own words and refer back to those notes as you move forward.

Many lessons in your math book include a prompt that asks you to think and write about the topic you are learning that day in a Learning Log. There is space in this Toolkit to write your Learning Log entries so that they are all in one place and are easy to use later. It is a good idea to leave some space between your entries so that you can add new ideas to them later, as you learn more. Note that this space has a light grid, which you can use like lined paper, as well as to help you draw diagrams or graphs.

Throughout the year, remember to make notes in your Toolkit and add examples if you find them helpful. It is important that the information on these pages—especially the Math Notes—makes sense to *you*, so be sure to highlight key information, write down important things to remember, and ask questions if something does not make sense.

Also remember that the information in your Toolkit can help you solve problems and keep track of important vocabulary words. Keep your Toolkit with you when you are working on math problems, and use it as a source of information as you move through the course.

At the end of each chapter in your textbook, there are lists of all of the Learning Log entries and Math Notes for that chapter. There are also lists of important vocabulary words. Take time as you complete each chapter to look through your Toolkit and make sure it is complete. Updating your Toolkit regularly and using it when you are studying are important student habits that will help you to be successful in this and future courses.

Have a wonderful year of learning!

The CPM Team

CHAPTER 1: INTRODUCTION AND PROBABILITY

Date: Lesson:	Learning Log Title:

Date: Lesson:	Learning Log Title:

Date: Lesson:	Learning Log Title:

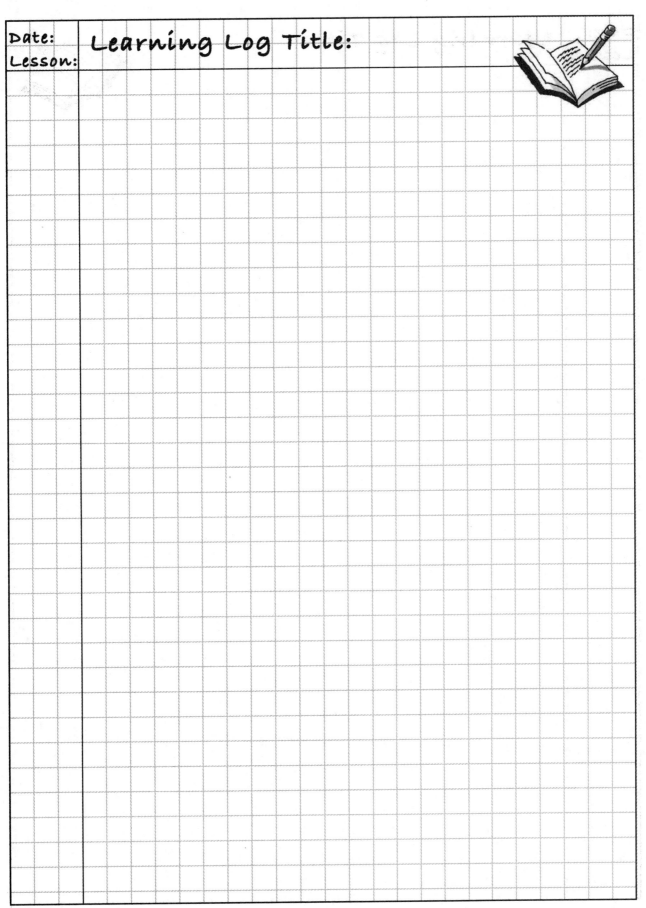

Date: Lesson:	Learning Log Title:

Date:	Learning Log Title:
Lesson:	

MATH NOTES

PERIMETER AND AREA

The **perimeter** of a shape is the total length of the boundary (around the shape) that encloses the interior (inside) region on a flat surface. See the examples at right.

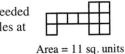

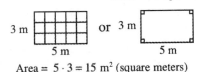

Perimeter = 20 units

Perimeter = $5 + 8 + 4 + 6 = 23$ cm

Area is a measure of the number of square units needed to cover a region on a flat surface. See the examples at right.

Area = 11 sq. units

The **area of a rectangle** is found by multiplying the lengths of the base and height. See the examples at right.

3 m [ ] or 3 m [ ]

5 m   5 m

Area = $5 \cdot 3 = 15$ m² (square meters)

$A = b \cdot h$

The **area of a parallelogram** is equal to the area of a rectangle with the same base and height. If the base of the parallelogram is length b and the height is length h, then the area of the parallelogram is $A = b \cdot h$.

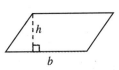

The **area of a triangle** is half the area of a parallelogram with the same base and height. If the base of the triangle is length b and the height length h, then the area of the triangle is $A = \frac{1}{2} b \cdot h$.

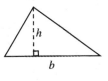

Finally, the **area of a trapezoid** is found by averaging the two bases and multiplying by the height. If the trapezoid has bases b_1 and b_2 and height h, then the area is: $A = \frac{1}{2}(b_1 + b_2)h$.

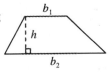

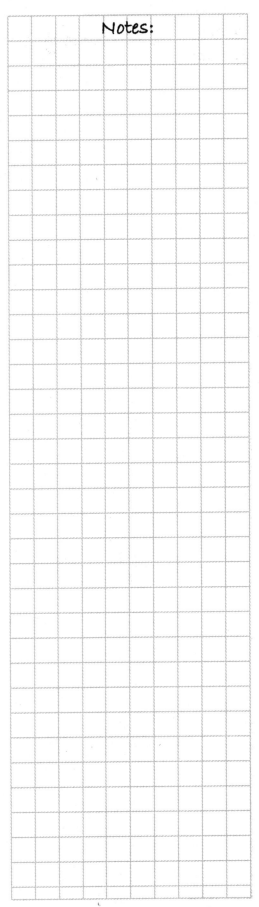

Notes:

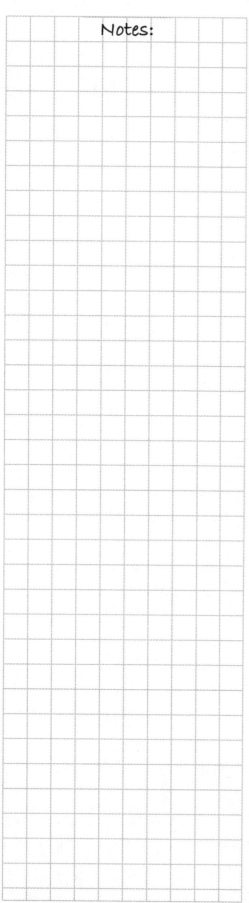

Notes:

MEAN

To understand a set of data, you often need to be able to describe the approximate "center" of that data. One way to do this is to find the **mean** of the data set, which is also called the **arithmetic average**.

To find the mean of a set of data, add the values of the data elements (numbers) and then divide by the number of items of data. The mean is a useful way to describe the data when the set of data does not contain **outliers**. Outliers are numbers that are much smaller or much larger than most of the other data in the set.

Suppose the following data set represents the number of home runs hit by the best seven players on a Major League Baseball team during one season:

$$16, 26, 21, 9, 13, 15, \text{ and } 9.$$

The mean is $\frac{16+26+21+9+13+15+9}{7} = \frac{109}{7} \approx 15.57$.

This number shows that a typical player among the best seven home-run hitters on the team hits about 15 or 16 home runs each season.

MEDIAN

The mean is a useful way to find the center when data values are close together or are evenly spaced. Another tool, the **median**, also locates the approximate "center" of a set of data in a different way.

The **median** is the middle number in a set of data *arranged numerically*. If there is an even number of values, the median is the mean of the two middle numbers. The median is more accurate than the mean as a way to find the center when there are outliers in the data set.

Suppose the following data set represents the number of home runs hit by the best seven players on a Major League Baseball team:

$$16, 26, 21, 9, 13, 15, \text{ and } 9.$$

In this example, the median is 15. This is because when the data are arranged in order (9, 9, 13, 15, 16, 21, 26), the middle number is 15. Mean and median are called **measures of central tendency** because they each describe the "center" of a set of data, but in different ways.

REPRESENTATIONS OF PROPORTIONS

The portions web diagram at right illustrates that fractions, decimals, and percents are different ways to represent a portion of a number. Portions can also be represented in words, such as "four-fifths" or "seven-fourths," or with diagrams such as those shown below. A complete portions web is shown below right.

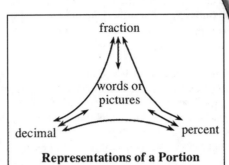

Representations of a Portion

150% of one circle is shaded:

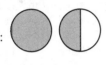

$\frac{4}{5}$ of the objects are shaded:

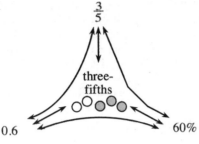

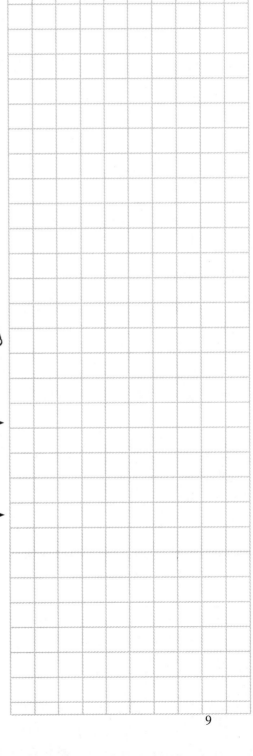

SCALING AXES

The numbers on each axis of a graph or a number line show the **scaling** of the axes. The difference between consecutive markings tells the size of the **interval**. When you scale each axis, you must use equal intervals to represent the data accurately. For example, an interval of 5 creates a scale numbered $-15, -10, -5, 0, 5, 10, 15$, etc. Unequal intervals distort the relationship in the data.

Notice on the graph at right that 80 marks the end of the *fourth* interval from zero on the horizontal axis. If you divide 80 years by 4 you can see that the length of an interval on this graph is 20.

$80 \div 4 = 20$

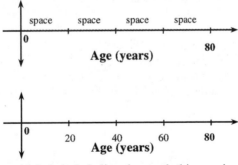

The second graph has each interval labeled. Labeling the graph this way is called "scaling the axis."

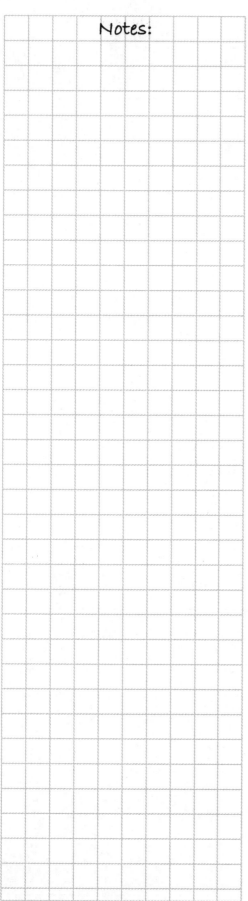

Notes:

PROBABILITY VOCABULARY AND DEFINITIONS

Outcome: Any possible or actual result of the action considered, such as rolling a 5 on a standard number cube or getting tails when flipping a coin.

Event: A desired (or successful) outcome or group of outcomes from an experiment, such as rolling an even number on a standard number cube.

Sample space: All possible outcomes of a situation. For example, the sample space for flipping a coin is heads and tails; rolling a standard number cube has six possible outcomes (1, 2, 3, 4, 5, and 6).

Probability: The likelihood that an event will occur. Probabilities may be written as fractions, decimals, or percents. An event that is guaranteed to happen has a probability of 1, or 100%. An event that has no chance of happening has a probability of 0, or 0%. Events that "might happen" have probabilities between 0 and 1 or between 0% and 100%. In general, the more likely an event is to happen, the greater its probability.

Experimental probability: The probability based on data collected in experiments.

$$\text{Experimental probability} = \frac{\text{number of successful outcomes in the experiment}}{\text{total number of outcomes in the experiment}}$$

Theoretical probability is a calculated probability based on the possible outcomes when they all have the same chance of occurring.

$$\text{Theoretical probability} = \frac{\text{number of successful outcomes (events)}}{\text{total number of possible outcomes}}$$

In the context of probability, "successful" usually means a desired or specified outcome (event), such as rolling a 2 on a number cube (probability of $\frac{1}{6}$). To calculate the probability of rolling a 2, first figure out how many possible outcomes there are. Since there are six faces on the number cube, the number of possible outcomes is 6. Of the six faces, only one of the faces has a 2 on it. Thus, to find the probability of rolling a 2, you would write:

$$P(2) = \frac{\text{number of ways to roll 2}}{\text{number of possible outcomes}} = \frac{1}{6} . \text{ or } 0.1\overline{6} \text{ .or approximately } 16.7\%$$

MULTIPLICATIVE IDENTITY

If any number or expression is multiplied by the number 1, the number or expression does not change. The number 1 is called the **multiplicative identity**. So, for any number x $1 \cdot x = x \cdot 1 = x$.

One way the multiplicative identity is used to create equivalent fractions using a Giant One.

$$\frac{2}{3} \cdot \boxed{\frac{2}{2}} = \frac{4}{6}$$

By multiplying a fraction by a fraction equivalent to 1, a new, equivalent fraction is created.

EQUIVALENT FRACTIONS

Fractions that are equal, but written in different forms, are called **equivalent fractions**. Rewriting a fraction in an equivalent form is useful when you want to compare two fractions or when you want to combine portions that are divided into pieces of different sizes.

A Giant One is a useful tool to create an equivalent fraction. To rewrite a fraction in a different form, multiply the original fraction by a fraction equivalent to 1. For example:

$$\frac{2}{3} \cdot \boxed{\frac{4}{4}} = \frac{2 \cdot 4}{3 \cdot 4} = \frac{8}{12}$$

A picture can also demonstrate that these two fractions are equivalent:

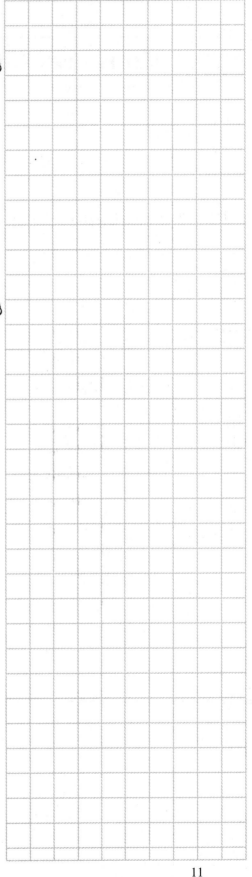

Notes:

CHAPTER 2: FRACTIONS AND INTEGER ADDITION

Date: Lesson:	Learning Log Title:

Date:	Learning Log Title:
Lesson:	

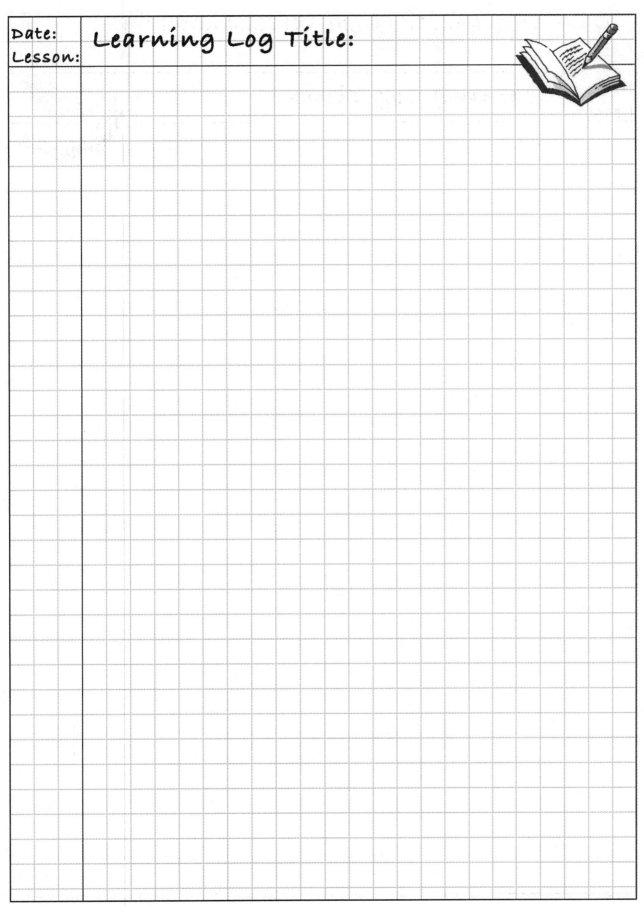

Date: Lesson:	Learning Log Title:

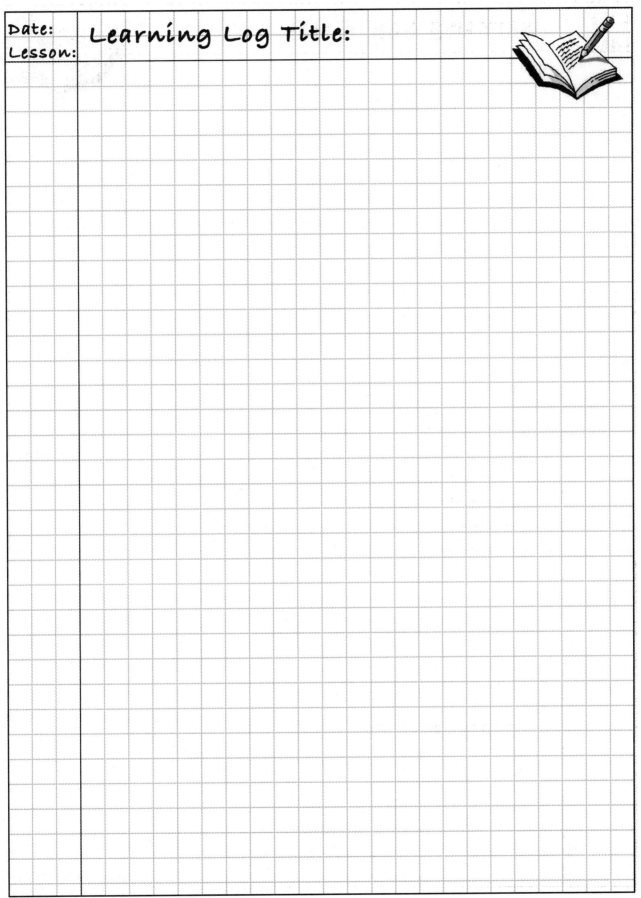

Date:
Lesson:

Learning Log Title:

Date:	Learning Log Title:
Lesson:	

MATH NOTES

MIXED NUMBERS AND FRACTIONS GREATER THAN ONE

The number $4\frac{1}{3}$ is called a **mixed number** because it is composed of a whole number, 4, and a fraction, $\frac{1}{3}$.

The number $\frac{13}{3}$ is a called a **fraction greater than one** because the numerator is larger than the denominator and its value is therefore greater than one. It is equal to the mixed number $4\frac{1}{3}$. Sometimes fractions greater than one are called *improper fractions*, but this is just a historical term. There is nothing actually wrong with the fraction.

Whether to write a number as a mixed number or a fraction greater than one depends on what arithmetic operation(s) you are performing. For some arithmetic operations, especially multiplication and division, you will usually want to write mixed numbers as fractions greater than one.

Fraction ⇔ Decimal ⇔ Percent

The **Representations of a Portion web** diagram at right illustrates that fractions, decimals, and percents are different ways to represent a portion of a number. Portions can also be represented in words, such as "four fifths" or "twelve-fifteenths" or with diagrams.

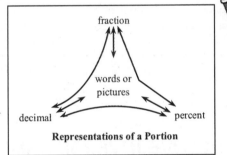

Representations of a Portion

Decimal to percent:
Multiply the decimal by 100.
$(0.34)(100) = 34\%$

Percent to decimal:
Divide the percent by 100.
$78.6\% = 78.6 \div 100 = 0.786$

Fraction to percent:
Set up an equivalent fraction using 100 as the denominator. The numerator is the percent.
$\frac{4}{5} \cdot \frac{20}{20} = \frac{80}{100} = 80\%$

Percent to fraction:
Use 100 as the denominator. Use the number in the percent as the numerator. Simplify as needed.
$22\% = \frac{22}{100} \cdot \frac{1/2}{1/2} = \frac{11}{50}$

Terminating decimal to fraction:
Use the digits as the numerator. Use the decimal place value as the denominator. Simplify as needed.
$0.2 = \frac{2}{10} = \frac{1}{5}$

Repeating decimal to fraction:
Count the number of decimal places in the repeating block. Write the repeating block as the numerator. Then, write the power of 10 for the number of places in the block, less 1, as the denominator. Below, the repeating block (713) has 3 decimal places so 713 is the numerator and $1000 - 1$ is the denominator.
$0.\overline{713} = \frac{713}{1000-1} = \frac{713}{999}$

Fraction to decimal:
Divide the numerator by the denominator.
$\frac{3}{8} = 3 \div 8 = 0.375$

MULTIPLICATION USING GENERIC RECTANGLES

To prepare for later topics in this course and future courses it is helpful to use an area model or generic rectangle to represent multiplication.

For the problem 67 • 46, think of 67 as 60 + 7 and 46 as 40 + 6. Use these numbers as the dimensions of a large rectangle as shown at right. Determine the area of each of the smaller rectangles and then find the sum of the four smaller areas. This sum is the answer to the original problem.

	60	7
40	2400	280
6	360	42

$$67 \cdot 46 = (60 + 7)(40 + 6) = 2400 + 280 + 360 + 42 = 3082$$

INTEGERS

Integers are positive and negative whole numbers and zero. On a number line, think of integers as "whole steps or no steps" in either direction from 0.

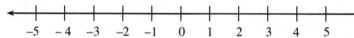

ADDITIVE INVERSE AND ADDITIVE IDENTITY

The **additive identity** is the number zero (0). When you add zero to any number, you get the same number you started with. For example, $3 + 0 = 3$. In general, $x + 0 = x$.

The **additive inverse** of a number is its opposite. For example, the additive inverse of 7 is –7 and the additive inverse of –2 is 2. The additive inverse "undoes" addition. Suppose you have the number 3 and you want to add a number to it to get zero (the additive identity). Then adding –3 gives you $3 + (-3) = 0$. Thus, –3 is the additive inverse of 3, and 3 is the additive inverse of –3. In general, $x + (-x) = 0$.

Notes:

ADDITION OF INTEGERS

Recall that **integers** are positive and negative whole numbers and zero, that is, $\ldots -3, -2, -1, 0, 1, 2, 3, \ldots$.

You have been introduced to two ways to think about addition. Both of them involve figuring out which, if any, parts of the numbers combine to form zero. One way to think about this concept is to think about the tightrope walker from problem 2-31. If Cecil travels one foot to the right (+1) and one foot to the left (–1), he will end up where he started, so the sum of (+1) and (–1) is zero.

Another useful strategy for finding zero is to use + and – tiles. The diagram at right can be represented by the equation $-1 + 1 = 0$. You can use this same idea for **adding any two integers**. Use + and – tiles to build the first integer, add the tiles for the second integer, and then eliminate zeros. Study the examples shown in the diagrams below.

Example 1: $5 + (-3)$ $+$ $+$ $5 + (-3) = 2$

Example 2: $-5 + (2)$ $-$ $-$ $-$ $-5 + (2) = -3$

Example 3: $-6 + (-2)$ $-6 + (-2) = -8$

With practice, zeros can be visualized. This helps you determine how many remaining positive or negative tiles show the simplified expression.

MULTIPLYING FRACTIONS USING A RECTANGLE

One way to model multiplying fractions is to shade a unit rectangle. Below is an example of shading a unit rectangle to represent $\frac{2}{3}$ of $\frac{2}{5}$ or, written as multiplication, $\frac{2}{3} \cdot \frac{2}{5}$.

Step 1: Divide a rectangle into five sections ("fifths") — the denominator of the second fraction. (Notice that the second number has been drawn first.)

Step 2: Shade horizontal sections to represent how many fifths there are — the numerator of the second fraction.

Step 3: Divide the rectangle vertically using the denominator of the other factor ("thirds").

Step 4: Use a darker shading to show how many thirds there are. For this example, shade two-thirds of the two-fifths.

Step 5: The product's numerator is the number of sections that are double-shaded. The product's denominator is the total number of sections in the rectangle. Write an equation to show the product: $\frac{2}{3} \cdot \frac{2}{5} = \frac{4}{15}$. Simplify or reduce the product when possible.

MULTIPLYING MIXED NUMBERS

Method 1: Using a generic rectangle.

To multiply mixed numbers, you may use a generic rectangle (based on the Distributive Property).

Example: $2\frac{1}{2} \cdot 1\frac{1}{4}$

$(2 + \frac{1}{2}) \cdot (1 + \frac{1}{4}) = 2 + \frac{2}{4} + \frac{1}{2} + \frac{1}{8}$

$\qquad = 2 + \frac{1}{2} + \frac{1}{2} + \frac{1}{8}$

$\qquad = 2 + 1 + \frac{1}{8}$

$\qquad = 3\frac{1}{8}$

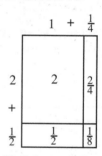

Find the area of each small rectangle.

Method 2: Using fractions greater than one. To multiply mixed numbers, first change them to fractions greater than one. Then multiply and write the result as a mixed number, if possible.

Example:

$2\frac{1}{2} \cdot 1\frac{1}{4}$

$\frac{5}{2} \cdot \frac{5}{4}$

$\frac{25}{8}$

$3\frac{1}{8}$

INTERVALS AND SCALING

The numbers on the axes of a graph show the **scaling** of the axes. The difference between consecutive markings tells the size of the **interval**. When you scale each axis, you must use equal intervals to represent the data accurately. For example, an interval of 5 creates a scale numbered 0, 5, 10, 15, etc. Unequal intervals distort the relationship in the data. It is important to note that horizontal and vertical axes *do not* need the same scaling. In fact, it is often convenient to choose different scales for the two axes.

Notice on the graph at right that 80 marks the end of the *fourth* interval. If you divide 80 years by 4, you can see that the length of an interval on this graph is 20.

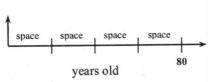

years old

$$(80 \div 4 = 20)$$

The second graph at right has each interval labeled. This is called "scaling the axis."

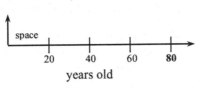

years old

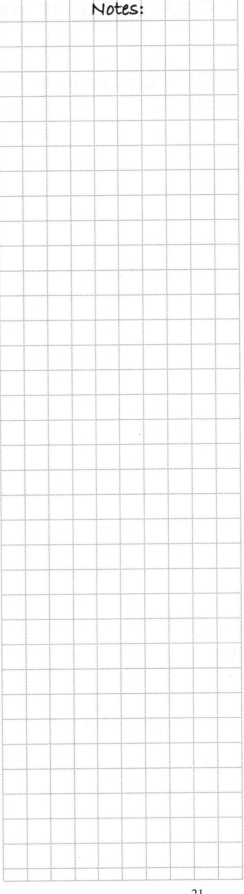

CHAPTER 3: ARITHMETIC PROPERTIES

Date: Lesson:	Learning Log Title:

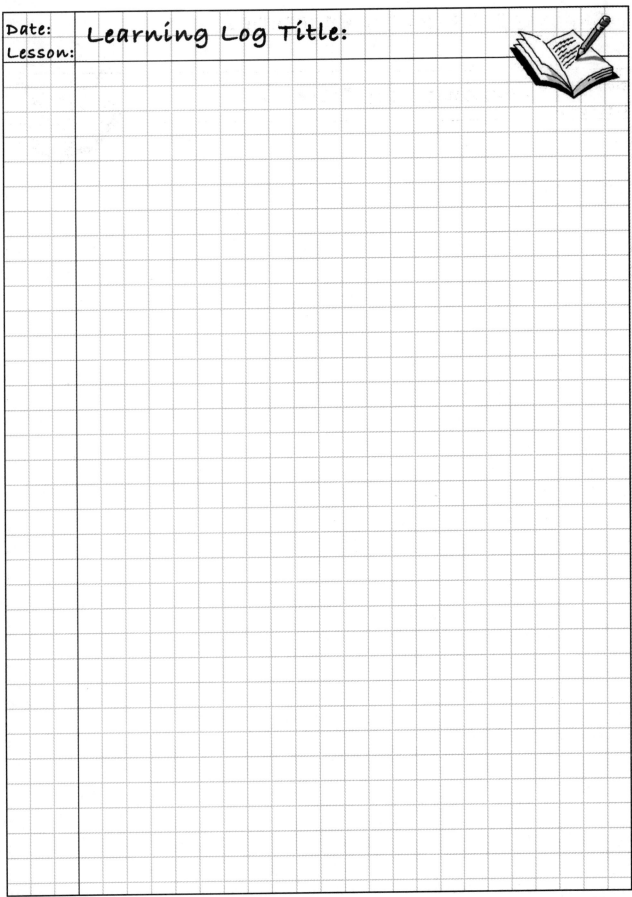

Date:
Lesson:

Learning Log Title:

| Date: | Learning Log Title: |
| Lesson: | |

Date: Lesson:	Learning Log Title: 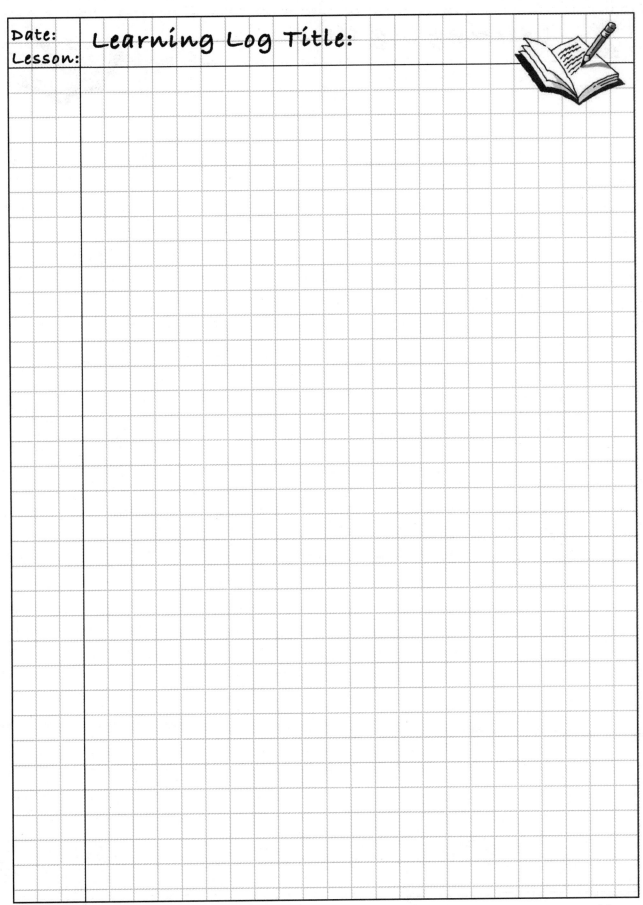

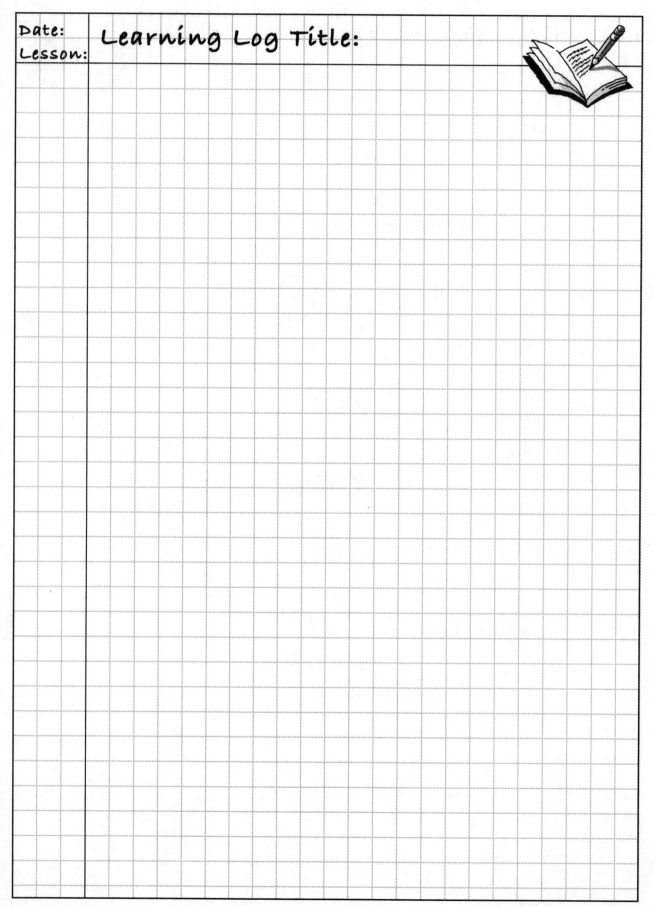

| Date: | Learning Log Title: |
| Lesson: | |

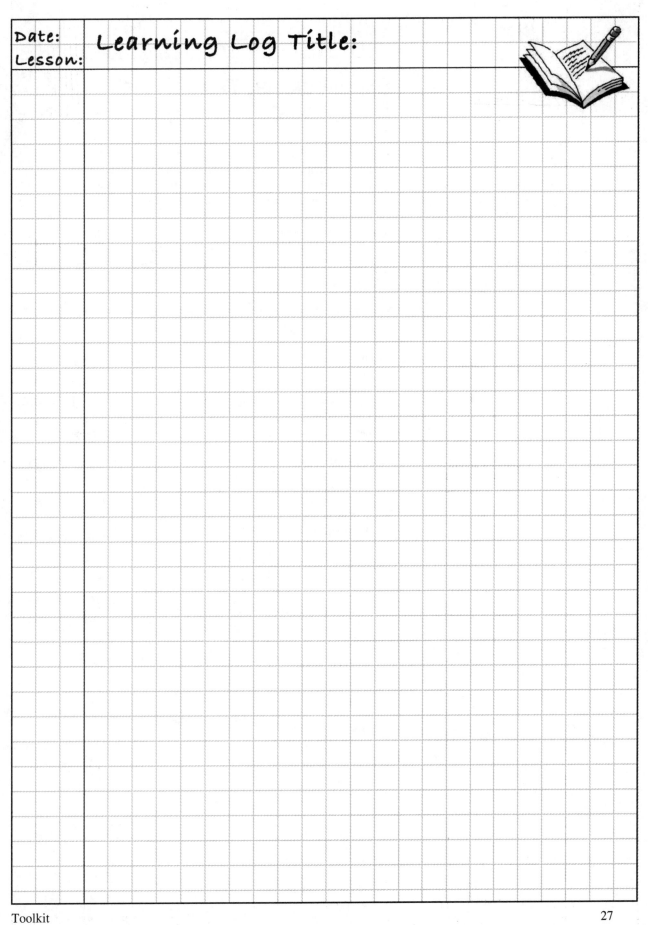

Date:

Lesson:

Learning Log Title:

MATH NOTES

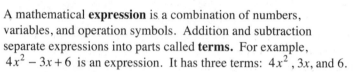

EXPRESSIONS, TERMS, AND ORDER OF OPERATIONS

A mathematical **expression** is a combination of numbers, variables, and operation symbols. Addition and subtraction separate expressions into parts called **terms.** For example, $4x^2 - 3x + 6$ is an expression. It has three terms: $4x^2$, $3x$, and 6.

A more complex expression is $2x + 3(5 - 2x) + 8$, which also has three terms: $2x$, $3(5 - 2x)$, and 8. But the term $3(5 - 2x)$ has another expression, $5 - 2x$, inside the parentheses. The terms of this expression are 5 and $2x$.

Mathematicians have agreed on an **order of operations** simplifying expressions.

Original expression:

$$(10 - 3 \cdot 2) \cdot 2^2 - \frac{13 - 3^2}{2} + 6$$

Circle expressions that are grouped within parentheses or by a fraction bar:

$$\boxed{(10 - 3 \cdot 2)} \cdot 2^2 - \boxed{\frac{13 - 3^2}{2}} + 6$$

Simplify *within* circled terms using the order of operations:

$$\boxed{(10 - 3 \cdot 2)} \cdot 2^2 - \boxed{\frac{13 - 3 \cdot 3}{2}} + 6$$

    Evaluate exponents.

$$\boxed{(10 - 6)} \cdot 2^2 - \boxed{\frac{13 - 9}{2}} + 6$$

    Multiply and divide from left to right.

$$(4) \cdot 2^2 - \frac{4}{2} + 6$$

    Combine terms by adding and subtracting from left to right.

$$\boxed{4 \cdot 2^2} - \boxed{\frac{4}{2}} + \boxed{6}$$

Circle the remaining terms:

$$\boxed{4 \cdot 2 \cdot 2} - \boxed{\frac{4}{2}} + \boxed{6}$$

Simplify *within* circled terms using the order of operations as described above:

$$16 - 2 + 6$$

$$20$$

EVALUATING ALGEBRAIC EXPRESSIONS

An **algebraic expression** consists of one or more variables, or a combination of numbers and variables connected by mathematical operations. Examples of algebraic expressions include $4x$, $3(x-5)$, and $4x-3y+7$.

To **evaluate** an algebraic expression for particular values of the variables, replace the variables in the expression with their known numerical values and simplify. Replacing variables with their known values is called **substitution**. An example is provided below.

Evaluate $4x-3y+7$ for $x=2$ and $y=1$.

Replace x and y with their known values of 2 and 1, respectively, and simplify.

$$4(2)-3(1)+7$$
$$=8-3+7$$
$$=12$$

SUBTRACTING INTEGERS

One method of adding integers, mentioned in a previous Math Notes box, was to start with a diagram of the first integer, add the second integer to the diagram, eliminate zeros, and then record what is left. One method of subtracting integers is to do the same, except that instead of adding the second integer, you remove the second integer. Sometimes this removal will require adding extra zeros to the diagram. Look at the examples below:

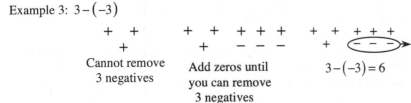

Example 1: $-3-(-2)$

Remove 2 negatives

$-3-(-2)=-1$

Example 2: $-5-(2)$

Cannot remove 2 positives

Add zeros until you can remove 2 positives

$-5-(2)=-7$

Example 3: $3-(-3)$

Cannot remove 3 negatives

Add zeros until you can remove 3 negatives

$3-(-3)=6$

Notes:

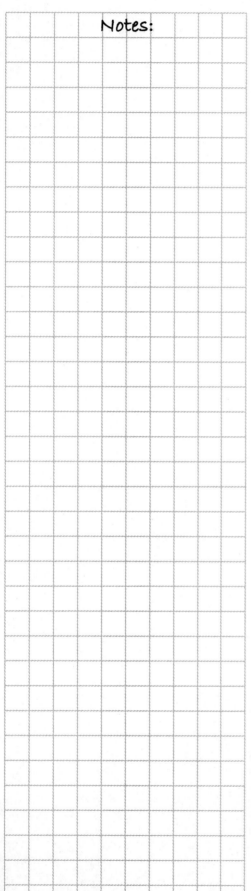

Notes:

CONNECTING ADDITION AND SUBTRACTION OF INTEGERS

Another method for subtracting integers is to notice the relationship between addition problems and subtraction problems, as shown below:

$$-3 - (-2) = -1 \quad \text{and} \quad -3 + 2 = -1$$
$$-5 - (2) = -7 \quad \text{and} \quad -5 + (-2) = -7$$
$$3 - (-3) = 6 \quad \text{and} \quad 3 + 3 = 6$$
$$2 - (-8) = 10 \quad \text{and} \quad 2 + 8 = 10$$

These relationships happen because removing a negative amount gives an identical result to adding the same positive amount and vice versa. The result of subtraction of two integers is the same as the result of the addition of the first integer and the *opposite* (more formally, the **additive inverse**) of the second integer.

Example 1: $-2 - (7) = -2 + (-7) = -9$

Example 2: $2 - (-3) = 2 + (3) = 5$

Example 3: $-8 - (-5) = -8 + (5) = -3$

Example 4: $2 - (9) = 2 + (-9) = -7$

Multiplication of Integers

Multiplication by a positive integer can be represented by combining groups of the same number:

$$(4)(3) = 3 + 3 + 3 + 3 = 12 \quad \text{and} \quad (4)(-3) = -3 + (-3) + (-3) + (-3) = -12$$

In both examples, the 4 indicates the number of groups of 3 (first example) and –3 (second example) to combine.

Multiplication by a negative integer can be represented by removing groups of the same number:

$$(-4)(3) = -(3) - (3) - (3) - (3) = -12$$
means "remove four groups of 3."

$$(-4)(-3) = -(-3) - (-3) - (-3) - (-3) = 12$$
means "remove four groups of –3."

In all cases, if there are an *even* number of negative factors to be multiplied, the product is *positive*; if there are an *odd* number of negative factors to be multiplied, the product is *negative*.

This rule also applies when there are more than two factors. Multiply the first pair of factors, then multiply that result by the next factor, and so on, until all factors have been multiplied.

$$(-2)(3)(-3)(-5) = -90 \quad \text{and} \quad (-1)(-1)(-2)(-6) = 12$$

MULTIPLICATIVE INVERSES AND RECIPROCALS

Two numbers with a product of 1 are called **multiplicative inverses**.

$$\frac{8}{5} \cdot \frac{5}{8} = \frac{40}{40} = 1 \qquad 3\frac{1}{4} = \frac{13}{4}, \text{ so } 3\frac{1}{4} \cdot \frac{4}{13} = \frac{13}{4} \cdot \frac{4}{13} = \frac{52}{52} = 1 \qquad \frac{1}{7} \cdot 7 = 1$$

In general $a \cdot \frac{1}{a} = 1$ and $\frac{a}{b} \cdot \frac{b}{a} = 1$, where neither a nor b equals zero. You can say that $\frac{1}{a}$ is the **reciprocal** of a and $\frac{b}{a}$ is the reciprocal of $\frac{a}{b}$. Note that 0 has no reciprocal.

DIVISION WITH FRACTIONS

Method 1: Using diagrams.

To divide by a fraction using a diagram, create a model of the situation using rectangles, a linear model, or a visual representation of it. Then break that model into the fractional parts named.

For example, to divide $\frac{7}{8} \div \frac{1}{2}$, you can draw the diagram at right to visualize how many $\frac{1}{2}$-sized pieces fit into $\frac{7}{8}$. The diagram shows that one $\frac{1}{2}$ fits, with $\frac{3}{8}$ of a whole left. Since $\frac{3}{8}$ is $\frac{3}{4}$ of $\frac{1}{2}$, you can see that $1\frac{3}{4}$ $\frac{1}{2}$-sized pieces fit into $\frac{7}{8}$, so $\frac{7}{8} \div \frac{1}{2} = 1\frac{3}{4}$.

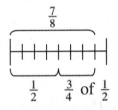

$$\frac{1}{2} \qquad \frac{3}{4} \text{ of } \frac{1}{2}$$

Method 2: Using common denominators.

To divide a number by a fraction using common denominators, express both numbers as fractions with the same denominator. Then divide the first numerator by the second. An example is shown at right.

$$\frac{2}{5} \div \frac{3}{10} = \frac{4}{10} \div \frac{3}{10}$$
$$= \frac{4}{3}$$
$$= 1\frac{1}{3}$$

Method 3: Using a Super Giant One.

To divide by a fraction using a Super Giant One, write the two numbers (dividend and divisor) as a complex fraction with the dividend as the numerator and the divisor as the denominator. Use the reciprocal of the complex fraction's denominator to create a Super Giant One. Then simplify as shown in the following example.

$$\frac{3}{4} \div \frac{2}{5} = \frac{\frac{3}{4}}{\frac{2}{5}} \cdot \frac{\frac{5}{2}}{\frac{5}{2}} = \frac{\frac{3 \cdot 5}{4 \cdot 2}}{1} = \frac{3}{4} \cdot \frac{5}{2} = \frac{15}{8} = 1\frac{7}{8}$$

Division with fractions by the Super Giant One method can be generalized and named the **invert and multiply** method. To invert and multiply, multiply the first fraction (dividend) by the reciprocal (or multiplicative inverse) of the second fraction (divisor). If the first number is an integer, write it as a fraction with a denominator of 1. If it is a mixed number, write it as a fraction greater than one. Here is the same problem in the third example above solved using this method:

$$\frac{3}{4} \div \frac{2}{5} = \frac{3}{4} \cdot \frac{5}{2} = \frac{15}{8} = 1\frac{7}{8}$$

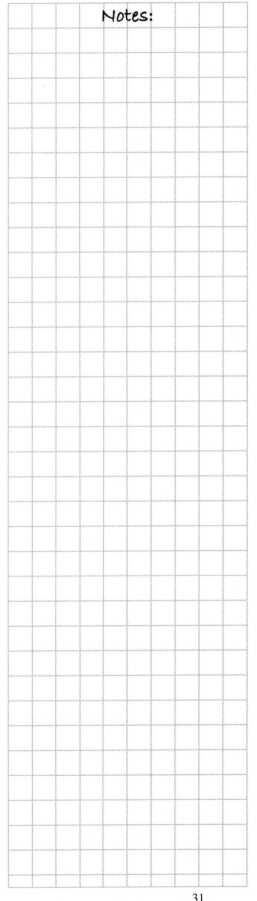

Notes:

MULTIPLYING DECIMAL NUMBERS

The answer to a multiplication problem is called the product of the factors. One way to place the decimal point correctly in the product is to count the decimal places in each of the factors. Then count that many places to the left from the farthest-right digit in the product.

Examples:

one place · two places = three places   1 + 2 places = 3 places

$$2.\underset{\sim}{3} \quad \cdot \quad 5.\underset{\sim}{06} \quad = \quad 11.\underset{\sim}{638}$$

four places · two places = six places   4 + 2 places = 6 places

$$0.\underset{\sim}{0004} \quad \cdot \quad 3.\underset{\sim}{42} \quad = 0.\underset{\sim}{001368}$$

DIVIDING DECIMAL NUMBERS

When you are dividing by a decimal number, one way to proceed is to count how many digits the decimal point must move to the right in the divisor so that it becomes an integer (whole number).

Then move the decimal point in the dividend the same direction and the same number of digits.

Example: $8.3 \div 4.07$

$$\text{divisor} \longrightarrow 4.\underset{\sim}{07} \overline{)8.\underset{\sim}{30} \uparrow} \longleftarrow \text{dividend}$$

Moving the decimal point two places to the right is the same as multiplying both numbers by 100.

The Giant One (Identity Property of Multiplication) illustrates this as shown below.

$$8.3 \div 4.07 = \frac{8.3}{4.07} \cdot \frac{100}{100} = \frac{830}{407}$$

CHAPTER 4: PROPORTIONS AND EXPRESSIONS

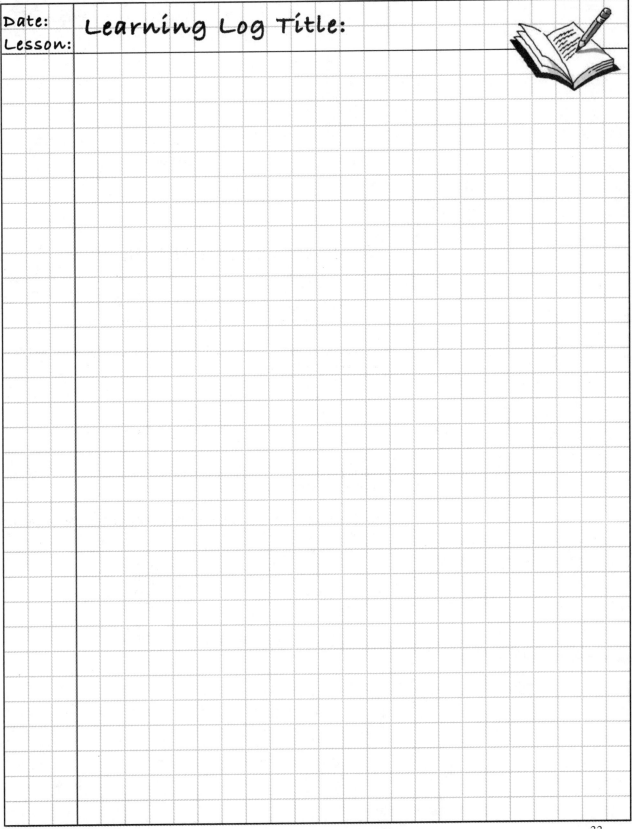

Date: Lesson:	Learning Log Title:

Date:	Learning Log Title:
Lesson:	

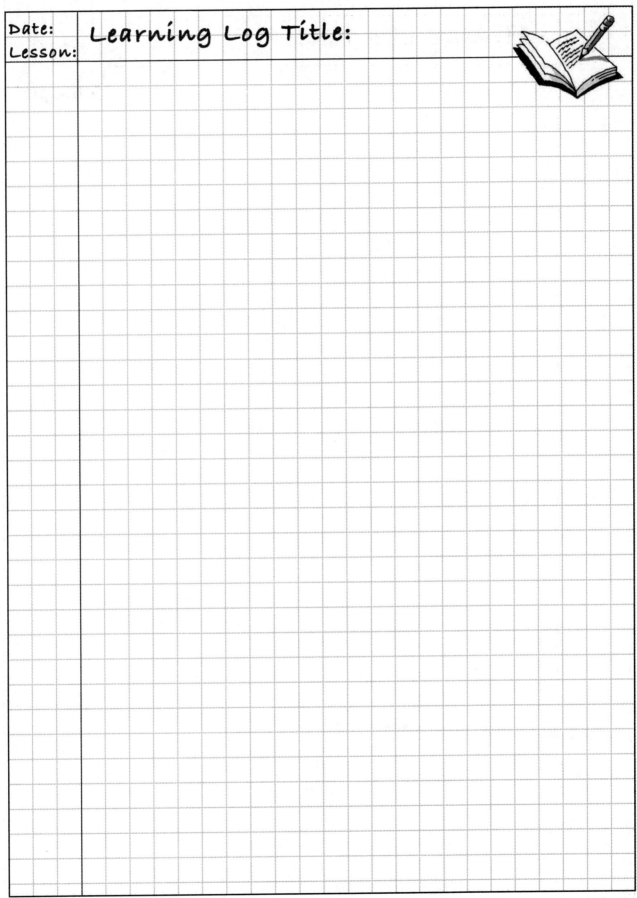

Date:
Lesson:

Learning Log Title:

Date:	Learning Log Title:
Lesson:	

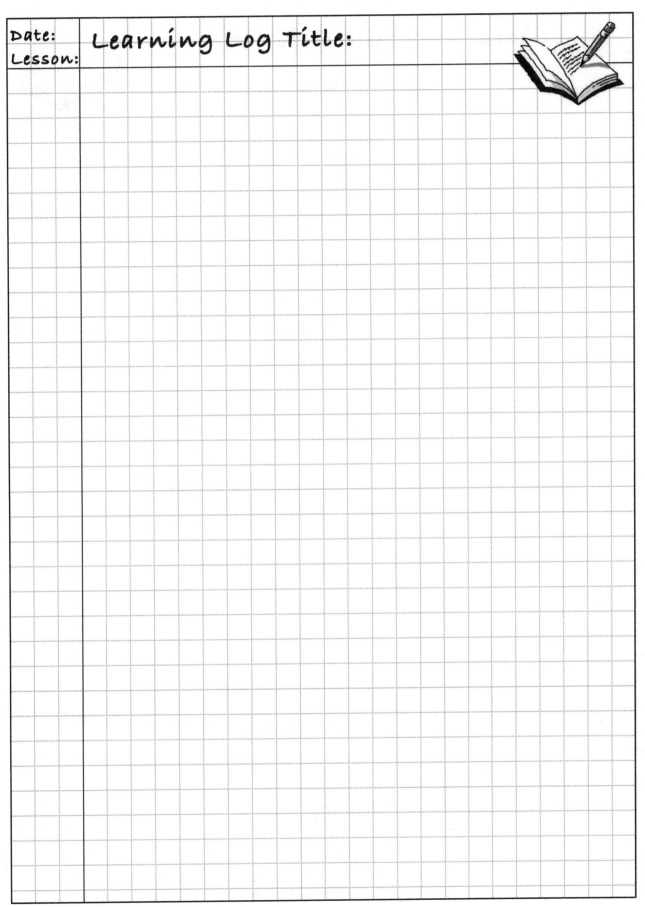

Date:

Lesson:

Learning Log Title:

MATH NOTES

MATHEMATICAL PROPERTIES

When two numbers or variables are combined using addition, the order in which they are added does not matter. For example, $7 + 5 = 5 + 7$. This fact is known as the **Commutative Property of Addition**.

Likewise, when two numbers are multiplied together, the order in which they are multiplied does not matter. For example, $5 \cdot 10 = 10 \cdot 5$. This fact is known as the **Commutative Property of Multiplication**.

These results can be generalized using variables:

$a + b = b + a$ and $a \cdot b = b \cdot a$

Note that subtraction and division do not satisfy the Commutative Property, since $7 - 5 \neq 5 - 7$ and $10 \div 5 \neq 5 \div 10$.

When three numbers are added, you usually add the first two of them and then add the third one to that result. However, you could also add the last two together and then add the first one to that result. The **Associative Property of Addition** tells you that the order in which the numbers are added together does not matter. The answer to the problem $(7 + 5) + 9$, for example, is the same as $7 + (5 + 9)$.

Likewise, when three numbers are multiplied together, which pair of numbers are multiplied together first does not matter. For example, $\big(5 \cdot (-6)\big) \cdot 10$ is the same as $5 \cdot (-6 \cdot 10)$. This is the **Associative Property of Multiplication**.

These results can be generalized using variables:

$(a + b) + c = a + (b + c)$ and $(a \cdot b) \cdot c = a \cdot (b \cdot c)$

Note that subtraction and division are *not* associative, since:

To multiply $8(24)$, written as $8(20 + 4)$, you can use the generic rectangle model at right.

The product is found by $8(20) + 8(4)$. So $8(20 + 4) = 8(20) + 8(4)$. This example illustrates the **Distributive Property**.

Symbolically, for any numbers a, b, and c: $a(b + c) = a(b) + a(c)$.

SIMILARITY

Two figures are **similar** if they have the same shape but not necessarily the same size. In similar figures, the lengths of all corresponding pairs of sides have the same ratio and the measures of corresponding angles are equal.

SCALE FACTOR

A **scale factor** compares the sizes of the parts of the scale drawing of an object with the actual sizes of the corresponding parts of the object itself. The scale factor in similar figures is the simplified ratio of any pair of corresponding sides.

Example:

$\frac{AB}{DE} = \frac{16}{40} = \frac{2}{5}$

$\frac{BC}{EF} = \frac{10}{25} = \frac{2}{5}$

$\frac{CA}{FD} = \frac{18}{45} = \frac{2}{5}$

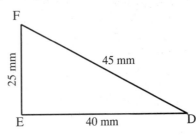

The simplified ratio of every pair of corresponding sides is the same. The scale factor is $\frac{2}{5}$.

PROPORTIONAL RELATIONSHIPS

A relationship is **proportional** if one quantity is a multiple of the other. This relationship can be identified in tables, graphs, and equations.

Table: Equivalent ratios of $\frac{y}{x}$ (or $\frac{x}{y}$) can be seen in a table.

Graph: A straight line through the origin.

Equation: An equation of the form $y = kx$ where k is the **constant of proportionality**.

Example: Three pounds of chicken cost $7.00. What is the cost for x pounds?

Equation: $y = \frac{7}{3} x$

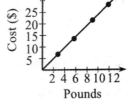

Pounds (x)	0	3	6	9	12
Cost (y)	0	7	14	21	28

The relationship between pounds and cost is proportional. The table has equivalent ratios ($\frac{7}{3} = \frac{14}{6} = \frac{21}{9}$), the graph is a straight line through the origin, and the equation is of the form $y = kx$.

Example: The county fair costs $5.00 to enter and $1.00 per ride.

Equation: $y = 1x + 5$

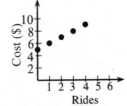

Rides (x)	0	1	2	3	4
Cost (y)	5	6	7	8	9

The relationship between rides and cost is not proportional, because the table does not contain equivalent ratios ($\frac{6}{1} \neq \frac{7}{2} \neq \frac{8}{3}$), the graph does not pass through the origin, and the equation contains addition.

Toolkit

Notes:

Notes:

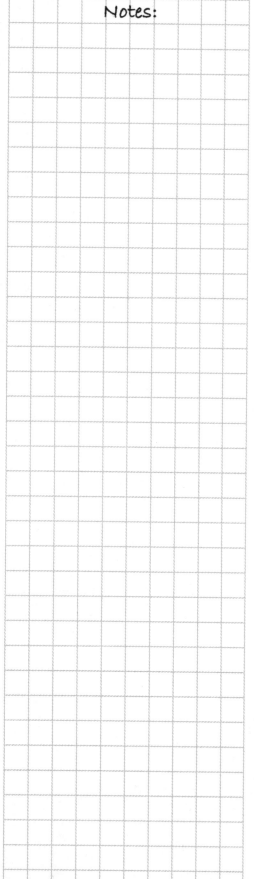

UNIT RATE

A **rate** is a ratio that compares, by division, the amount one quantity changes as another quantity changes.

$$\text{rate} = \frac{\text{change in one quantity}}{\text{change in another quantity}}$$

A **unit rate** is a rate that compares the change in one quantity to a one unit change in another quantity. For example, *miles per hour* is a unit rate, because it compares the change in miles to a change of one hour. If an airplane flies 3000 miles in 5 hours and uses 6000 gallons of fuel, you can compute several unit rates.

It uses $\frac{6000 \text{ gallons}}{5 \text{ hours}} = \frac{1200 \text{ gallons}}{1 \text{ hour}}$ or $\frac{6000 \text{ gallons}}{3000 \text{ miles}} = \frac{2 \text{ gallons}}{1 \text{ mile}}$.

It travels at $\frac{3000 \text{ miles}}{5 \text{ hours}} = \frac{600 \text{ miles}}{1 \text{ hour}}$.

NAMING ALGEBRA TILES

Algebra tiles help us represent unknown quantities in a concrete way. For example, in contrast to a 1×5 tile that has a length of 5 units, like the one shown at right, an x-tile has an unknown length. You can represent its length with a symbol or letter (like x) that represents a number, called a variable. Because its length is not fixed, the x-tile could be 6 units, 5 units, 0.37 units, or any other number of units long.

5 units

1 unit

x

1 unit ←Can be any length→

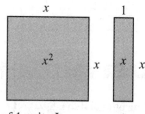

x 1

x^2 x x x

Algebra tiles can be used to build algebraic expressions. The three main algebra tiles are shown at right. The large square has a side of length x units. Its area is x^2 square units, so it is referred to as an x^2-tile.

The rectangle has length of x units and width of 1 unit. Its area is x square units, so it is called an x-tile.

1

1

The small square has a side of length 1 unit. Its area is 1 square unit, so it is called a one or unit tile. Note that the unit tile in this course will not be labeled with its area.

COMBINING LIKE TERMS

This course uses tiles to represent variables and single numbers (called **constant terms**). Combining tiles that have the same area to write a simpler expression is called **combining like terms**. See the example shown at right.

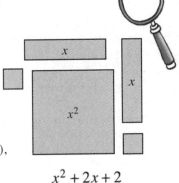

$$x^2 + 2x + 2$$

More formally, **like terms** are two or more terms that have the same variable(s), with the corresponding variable(s) raised to the same power.

Examples of like terms: $2x^2$ and $-5x^2$, $4ab$ and $3ab$.

Examples that are *not* like terms: 5 and $3x$, $5x$ and $7x^2$, a^2b and ab.

When you are not working with the actual tiles, it helps to visualize them in your mind. You can use the mental images to combine terms that are the same. Here are two examples:

Example 1: $2x^2 + x + 3 + x^2 + 5x + 2$ is equivalent to $3x^2 + 6x + 5$

Example 2: $3x^2 + 2x + 7 - 2x^2 - x + 7$ is equivalent to $x^2 + x + 14$

When several tiles are put together to form a more complicated figure, the area of the new figure is the sum of the areas of the individual pieces, and the perimeter is the sum of the lengths around the outside. Area and perimeter expressions can be **simplified**, or rewritten, by combining like terms.

For the figure at right, the perimeter is:
$x + 1 + x + 1 + 1 + 1 + 1 + 1 + x + x = 4x + 6$ units

DISTRIBUTIVE PROPERTY

The **Distributive Property** states that multiplication can be "distributed" as a multiplier of each term in a sum or difference. It is a method to separate or group quantities in multiplication problems. For example, $3(2 + 4) = 3 \cdot 2 + 3 \cdot 4$. Symbolically, it is written:

$$a(b + c) = ab + ac \text{ and } a(b - c) = ab - ac$$

For example, the collection of tiles at right can be represented as 4 sets of $x + 3$, written as $4(x + 3)$. It can also be represented by 4 x-tiles and 12 unit tiles, written as $4x + 12$.

4 sets of $x + 3$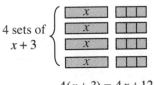

$$4(x + 3) = 4x + 12$$

Toolkit

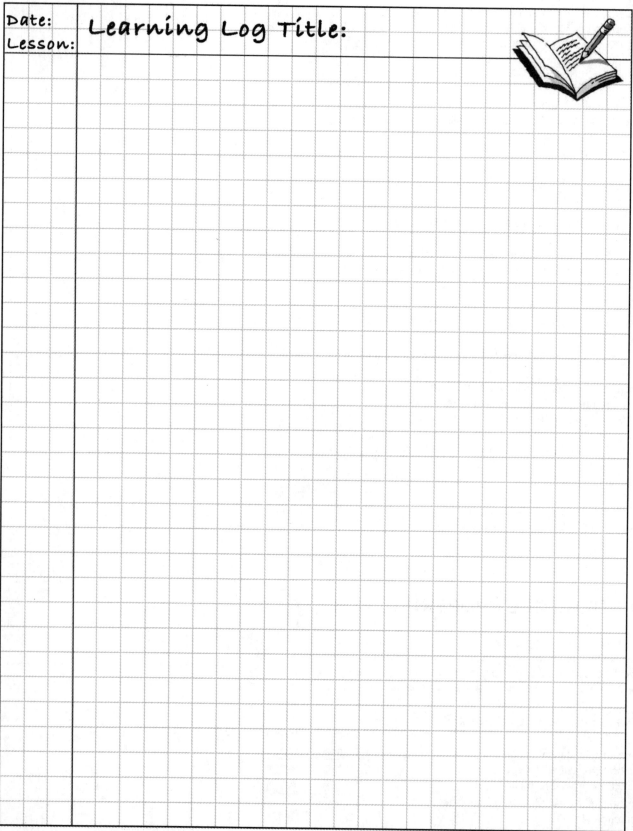

Date: Lesson:	Learning Log Title:

Date: Lesson:	Learning Log Title:

Date: Lesson:	Learning Log Title:

Date: Lesson:	Learning Log Title:

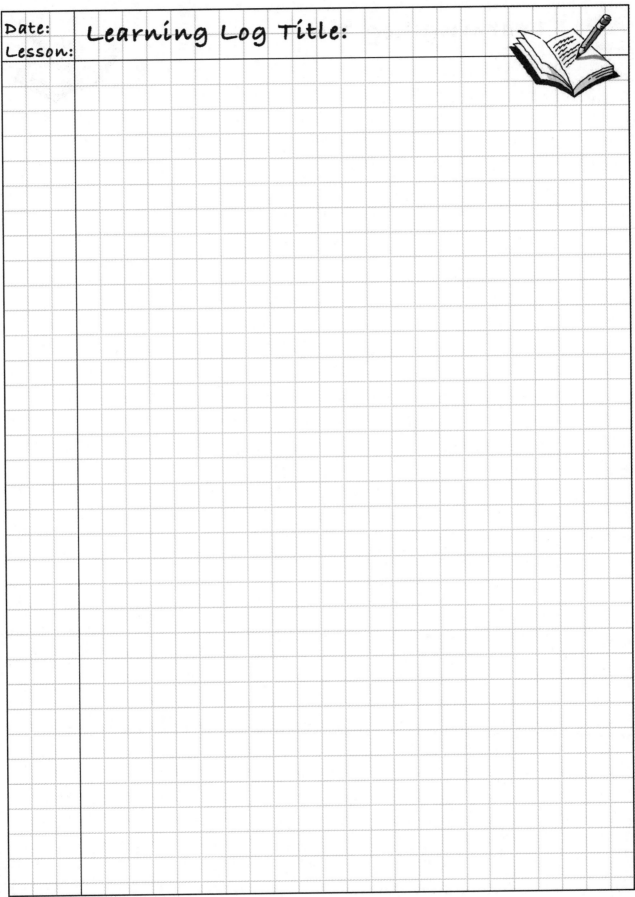

Date:	Learning Log Title:
Lesson:	

MATH NOTES

EQUIVALENT RATIOS

A **ratio** is a comparison of two quantities by division. A ratio can be written in words, as a fraction, or with colon notation. Most often in this course, ratios will be written as fractions or stated in words.

For example, if there are 28 students in a math class and 15 of them are girls, you can write the ratio of the number of girls to the number of students in the class as:

15 girls to 28 students $\dfrac{15 \text{ girls}}{28 \text{ students}}$ 15 girls : 28 students

You used a Giant One to write equivalent fractions in Chapter 1. To rewrite any ratio as an **equivalent ratio**, write it as a fraction and multiply it by a fraction equal to one. For example, you can show that the ratio of raisins to peanuts is the same for a larger mixture using a Giant One like this:

$$\frac{4 \text{ raisins}}{7 \text{ peanuts}} \cdot \frac{20}{20} = \frac{80 \text{ raisins}}{140 \text{ peanuts}}$$

Equivalent fractions (or ratios) can be thought of as families of fractions. There are an infinite number of fractions that are equivalent to a given fraction. You may want to review the basis for using a Giant One — the Multiplicative Identity — in the Math Notes box in Lesson 1.2.5.

Notes:

PART-TO-WHOLE RELATIONSHIPS

Percentages, fractions, and decimals are all different ways to represent a portion of a whole or a number. Portion-whole relationships can also be described in words.

You can represent a part-to-whole relationship with a linear model like the one below. To solve a percentage problem described in words, you must first identify three important quantities: the percent, the whole, and the part of the whole. One of the quantities will be unknown. A diagram can help you organize the information. For example:

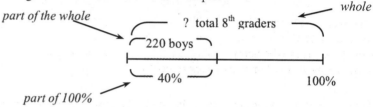

Once the parts have been identified, you can use reasoning to extend the part to the whole. For example, if 220 students are 40% of eighth graders, then 10% must be $220 \div 4 = 55$. Then 100% must be $55 \cdot 10 = 550$ students. Another way to solve the problem is to find the ratio of 220 boys to the whole (all students) and compare that ratio to 40% and 100%. This could be written:

$$\frac{40}{100} \cdot \boxed{} = \frac{220}{?} \text{ , then } \frac{40}{100} \cdot \boxed{\frac{5.5}{5.5}} = \frac{220}{?}$$

You can see above that the total number of 8th graders is 550.

To remember how to rewrite decimals or fractions as percents, and to rewrite percents as fractions or decimals, refer to the Math Notes box at the end of Lesson 1.3.1.

INDEPENDENT AND DEPENDENT EVENTS

Two events are **independent** if the outcome of one event does not affect the outcome of the other event. For example, if you draw a card from a standard deck of playing cards but replace it before you draw again, the outcomes of the two draws are independent.

Two events are **dependent** if the outcome of one event affects the outcome of the other event. For example, if you draw a card from a standard deck of playing cards and do not replace it for the next draw, the outcomes of the two draws are dependent.

PROBABILITY OF COMPOUND EVENTS

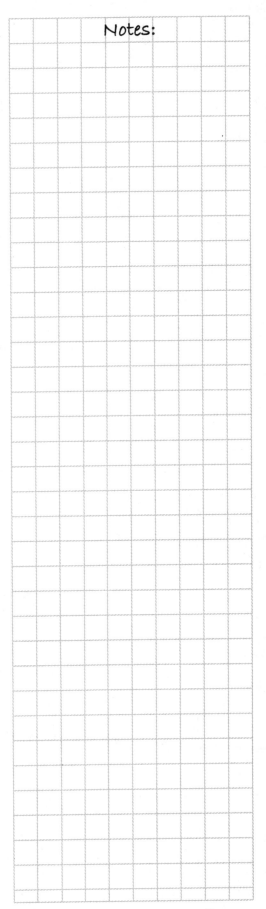

Sometimes when you are finding a probability, you are interested in either of two outcomes taking place, but not both. For example, you may be interested in drawing a king or a queen from a deck of cards. At other times, you might be interested in one event followed by another event. For example, you might want to roll a one on a number cube and then roll a six. The probabilities of combinations of simple events are called **compound events**.

To find the probability of *either* one event *or* another event that has nothing in common with the first, you can find the probability of each event separately and then add their probabilities. Using the example above of drawing a king or a queen from a deck of cards:

$$P(\text{king}) = \tfrac{4}{52} \quad \text{and} \quad P(\text{queen}) = \tfrac{4}{52} \quad \text{so} \quad P(\text{king or queen}) = \tfrac{4}{52} + \tfrac{4}{52} = \tfrac{8}{52} = \tfrac{2}{13}$$

For two independent events, to find the probability of *both* one *and* the other event occurring, you can find the probability of each event separately and then multiply their probabilities. Using the example of rolling a one followed by a six on a number cube:

$$P(1) = \tfrac{1}{6} \quad \text{and} \quad P(6) = \tfrac{1}{6} \quad \text{so} \quad P(1 \text{ then } 6) = \tfrac{1}{6} \cdot \tfrac{1}{6} = \tfrac{1}{36}$$

Note that you would carry out the same computation if you wanted to know the probability of rolling a one on a green cube and a six on a red cube if you rolled both of them at the same time.

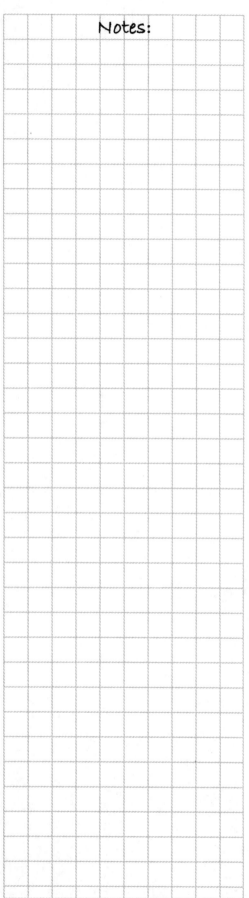

PROBABILITY MODELS FOR MULTIPLE EVENTS

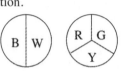

To determine all possible outcomes for multiple events when *both* one event *and* the other occur, there are several different models you can use to help organize the information.

Consider spinning each spinner at right once.

If you use a plan or a pattern to find all of the outcomes in an event, you are making a **systematic list**. For example, assume that you first spin B on spinner 1. Then, list all of the possible outcomes on spinner 2. Next, assume that your first spin is W on spinner 1, and complete the list.

Systematic List

BR	WR
BG	WG
BY	WY

A **probability table** can also organize information if there are exactly two events. The possibilities for each event are listed on the sides of the table as shown, and the combinations of outcomes are listed inside the table. In the example at right, the possible outcomes for spinner 1 are listed on the left side, and the possible outcomes for spinner 2 are listed across the top.

Probability Table

	R	G	Y
B	BR	BG	BY
W	WR	WG	WY

The possible outcomes of the two events are shown inside the rectangle. In this table, the top and side are divided evenly because the outcomes are equally likely. Inside the table you can see the possible combinations of outcomes.

A **probability tree** is another method for organizing information. The different outcomes are organized at the end of branches of a tree. The first section has B and W at the ends of two branches because there are two possible outcomes of spinner 1, namely B and W. Then the ends of three more branches represent the possible outcomes of the second spinner, R, G, and Y. These overall possible outcomes of the two events are shown as the six branch ends.

Probability Tree

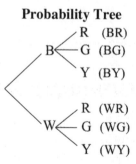

SOLVING PROBLEMS WITH THE 5-D PROCESS

The **5-D Process** is an organized method to solve problems. The D's stand for Describe/Draw, Define, Do, Decide, and Declare. An example of this work is shown below.

Problem: The base of a rectangle is 13 centimeters longer than the height. If the perimeter is 58 centimeters, find the base and the height of the rectangle.

Describe/Draw: The shape is a rectangle and we are looking at the perimeter.

height

base

Define		Do	Decide
Height (trial)	Base (height + 13)	Perimeter 2(base) + 2(height)	58?
Trial 1: 10	10 + 13 = 23	2(23) + 2(10) = 66	66 is too high

Use a trial value.   Use the relationships stated in the problem to determine the values of the other quantities (such as base and perimeter).

Decide if the answer is correct. Revise and make another trial until you find the correct answer.

Trial 3: 7	7 + 13 = 20	2(20) + 2(7) = 54	too low
Trial 2: 8	8 + 13 = 21	2(21) + 2(8) = 58	correct

Declare: The base is 21 centimeters and the height is 8 centimeters.

CONSECUTIVE INTEGERS

Consecutive integers are integers that come "one after another" in order (that is, without skipping any of them). For example: 11, 12, and 13 are three consecutive integers. The numbers 10, 12, 14, and 16 are four **consecutive even integers** because in counting up from 10, no even numbers are skipped. Likewise, 15, 17, and 19 are **consecutive odd integers**.

In algebra, it is sometimes necessary to represent a list of consecutive integers. To represent any list in general, you must use variables. It is common to let x represent the first integer. See the examples below of how to write a list of consecutive integers.

Three consecutive integers: $x, x+1, x+2$
Three consecutive odd integers: $x, x+2, x+4$
Three consecutive even integers: $x, x+2, x+4$

Note that consecutive even integers and odd integers look alike because both even integers and odd integers are two apart.

Toolkit

Date: Lesson:	Learning Log Title:

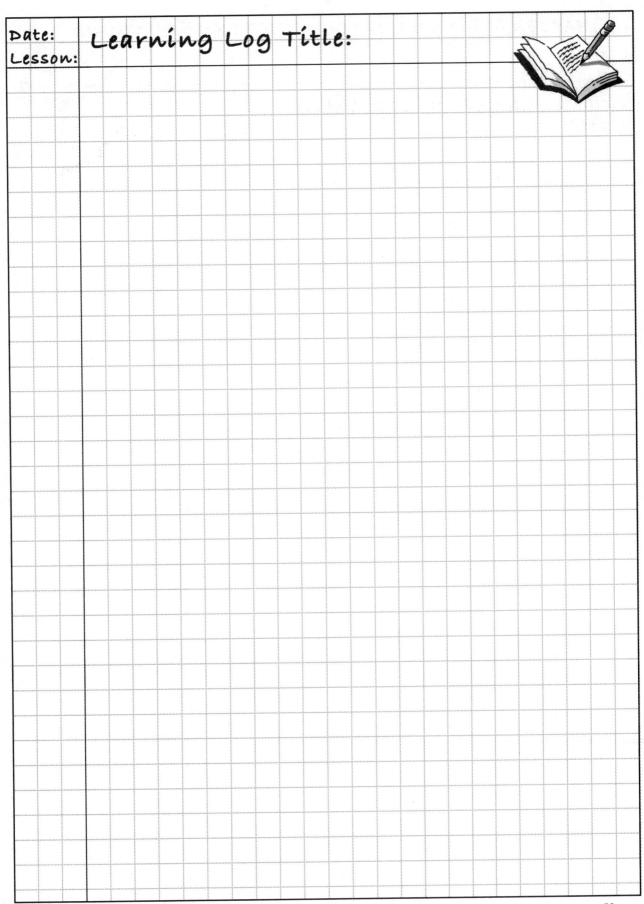

Date:	Learning Log Title:
Lesson:	

Date:	Learning Log Title:
Lesson:	

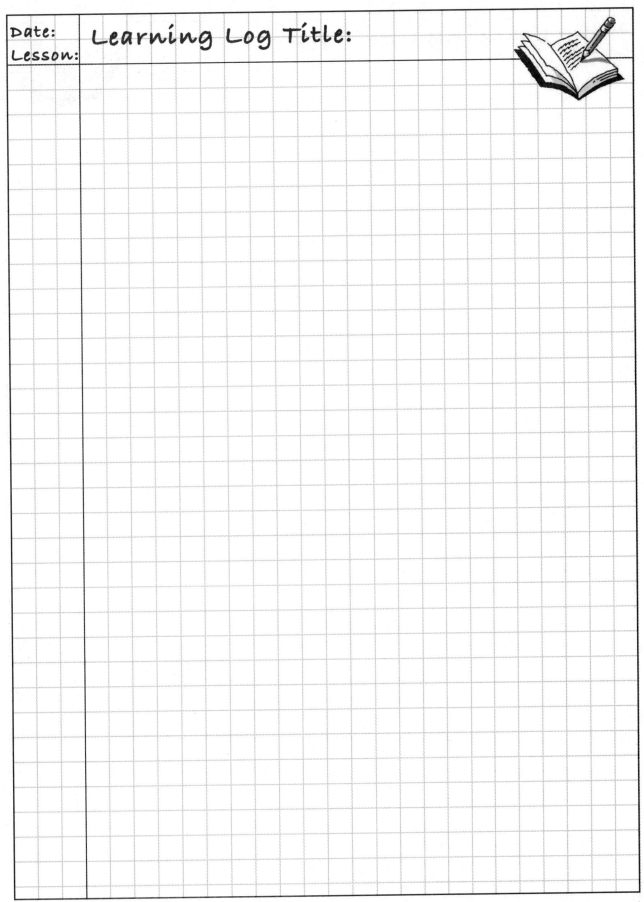

Date: Lesson:	Learning Log Title:

Date: Lesson:	Learning Log Title:

MATH NOTES

INEQUALITY SYMBOLS

Just as the symbol "=" is used in mathematics to represent that two quantities are equal, the **inequality symbols** at right are used to describe the relationships between quantities that are not necessarily equal. Examples: $3 < 7$, $14 \leq 14$, $-7 < -3$, $19 \geq 14$.

$<$ less than

$\leq$ less than or equal to

$>$ greater than

$\geq$ greater than or equal to

ALGEBRA VOCABULARY

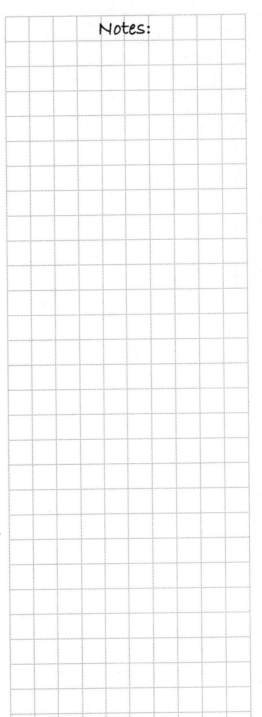

Variable: A letter or symbol that represents one or more numbers.

Expression: A combination of numbers, variables, and operation symbols. An expression does not contain an equal sign. For example, $2x + 3(5 - 2x) + 8$. Also, $5 - 2x$ is a smaller expression within the larger expression.

Term: Parts of the expression separated by addition and subtraction. For example, in the expression $2x + 3(5 - 2x) + 8$, the three terms are $2x$, $3(5 - 2x)$, and 8. The expression $5 - 2x$ has two terms, 5 and $2x$.

Coefficient: The numerical part of a term. In the expression $2x + 3(5 - 2x) + 8$, 2 is the coefficient of $2x$. In the expression $17x - 15x^2$, both 7 and 15 are coefficients.

Constant term: A number that is not multiplied by a variable. In the example above, 8 is a constant term. The number 3 is not a constant term because it is multiplied by a variable inside the parentheses.

Factor: Part of a multiplication expression. In the expression $3(5 - 2x)$, 3 and $5 - 2x$ are factors.

Notes:

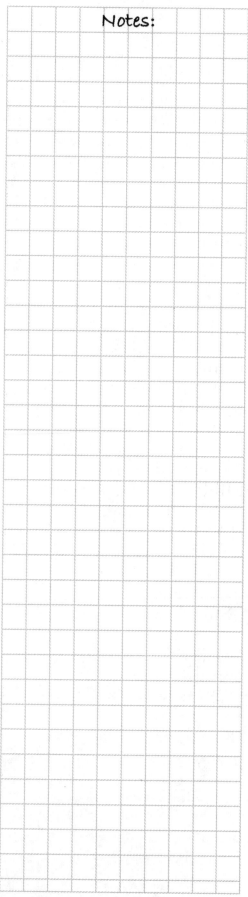

GRAPHING INEQUALITIES

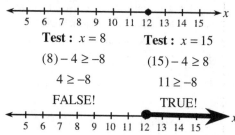

To solve and graph an inequality with one variable, first treat the problem as if it were an equality and solve the problem. The solution to the equality is called the **boundary point**. For example, to solve $x - 4 \geq 8$, first solve $x - 4 = 8$. The solution $x = 12$ is the boundary point for the inequality $x - 4 \geq 8$.

Since the original inequality is true when $x = 12$, place your boundary point on the number line as a solid point. Then test one value on either side in the *original* inequality by substituting it into the original inequality.

$$\textbf{Test}: x = 8$$
$$(8) - 4 \geq -8$$
$$4 \geq -8$$
$$\text{FALSE!}$$

$$\textbf{Test}: x = 15$$
$$(15) - 4 \geq 8$$
$$11 \geq -8$$
$$\text{TRUE!}$$

This will determine which set of numbers makes the inequality true. Write the inequality solution and extend an arrow onto the number line in the direction of the side that makes the inequality true. This is shown with the examples of $x = 8$ and $x = 15$ above. Therefore, the solution is $x \geq 12$ (also shown on the number line).

When the inequality is $<$ or $>$, the boundary point is *not* included in the answer. On a number line, this would be indicated with an open circle at the boundary point. For example, the graph of $x < 7$ is shown below.

USING AN EQUATION MAT

An **Equation Mat** can help you visually represent an equation with algebra tiles. It can also help you find the solution to an equation.

For example, the equation $2(x - 3) + x + 4 = 9 - 2x + 1 + x$ can be represented as shown on the first Equation Mat below. Then it can be solved using simplification steps (also know as legal moves) to show that the solution is $x = 3$.

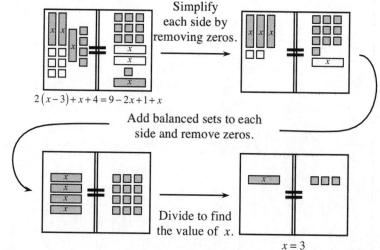

Simplify each side by removing zeros.

$2(x - 3) + x + 4 = 9 - 2x + 1 + x$

Add balanced sets to each side and remove zeros.

Divide to find the value of x.

$x = 3$

EQUATIONS AND INEQUALITIES

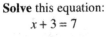

Equations always have an equal sign. **Inequalities** have one of inequality symbols defined in the Lesson 6.1.1 Math Note. To **solve** an equation or inequality means to find all values of the variable that make the relationship true. The solution can be shown on a number line. See the examples below.

Solve this equation:
$$x + 3 = 7$$
The solution is:
$$x = 4$$

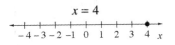

Solve this inequality:
$$x - 2 < 5$$
The solution is:
$$x < 7$$

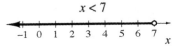

Notes:

CHECKING A SOLUTION

To check a solution to an equation, substitute the solution into the equation and verify that it makes the two sides of the equation equal.

For example, to verify that $x = 10$ is a solution to the equation $3(x - 5) = 15$, substitute 10 into the equation for x and then verify that the two sides of the equation are equal.

$$3(10 - 5) \overset{?}{=} 15$$
$$3(5) \overset{?}{=} 15$$
$$15 = 15$$

 True, so x = 10 is a solution.

$$3(2 - 5) \overset{?}{=} 15$$
$$3(-3) \overset{?}{=} 15$$
$$-9 \neq 15$$

 Not true, so x = 2 is not a solution.

As shown at right, $x = 10$ is a solution to the equation $3(x - 5) = 15$.

What happens when you do this check if your answer is incorrect? For example, try substituting $x = 2$ into the same equation. The result shows that $x = 2$ is not a solution to this equation.

DEFINING A VARIABLE

When you write an equation, it is important to **define the variable** carefully. You need to be clear about what you are talking about so that someone else looking at your work understands what the variable represents. This step is an important habit to develop because it is an important step in solving many different math problems.

For example, suppose you have this problem:

At the neighborhood grocery store, grapes cost $3 a pound. If Belinda spent $5.40 on grapes, how many pounds of grapes did she buy?

One equation you could write is $3x = 5.4$, if you know what x stands for. The variable x should be clearly defined, such as $x =$ pounds of grapes, rather than just $x =$ grapes. You could also write $g =$ pounds of grapes, since any letter may be used as a variable.

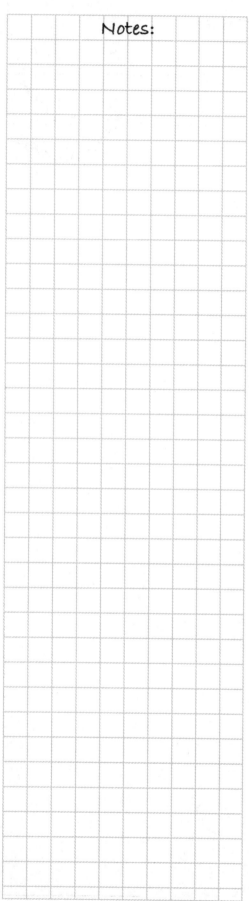

Notes:

SOLUTIONS TO AN EQUATION WITH ONE VARIABLE

A **solution** to an equation gives the value(s) of the variable that makes the equation true.

For example, when 5 is substituted for x in the equation at right, both sides of the equation are equal. Therefore, $x = 5$ is a solution to this equation. Some equations have several solutions, such as $x^2 = 25$, where $x = 5$ or -5.

$$4x - 1 = 2x + 9$$
$$4(5) - 1 = 2(5) + 9$$
$$19 = 19$$

Equations may also have no solution or an infinite (unlimited) number of solutions.

Notice that no matter what the value of x is, the left side of the first equation will never equal the right side. Therefore, it could be said that $x + 2 = x + 3$ has **no solution**.

Equation with no solution:
$$x + 2 = x + 3$$
$$2 \neq 3$$

However, in the equation $x - 2 = x - 2$, no matter what value x has, the equation will always be true. All numbers can make $x - 2 = x - 2$ true. Therefore, it could be said that the solution for the equation $x - 2 = x - 2$ is **all numbers**.

Equation with infinitely many solutions:
$$x - 2 = x - 2$$
$$-2 = -2$$

CHAPTER 7: PROPORTIONS AND PERCENTS

Date: Lesson:	Learning Log Title:

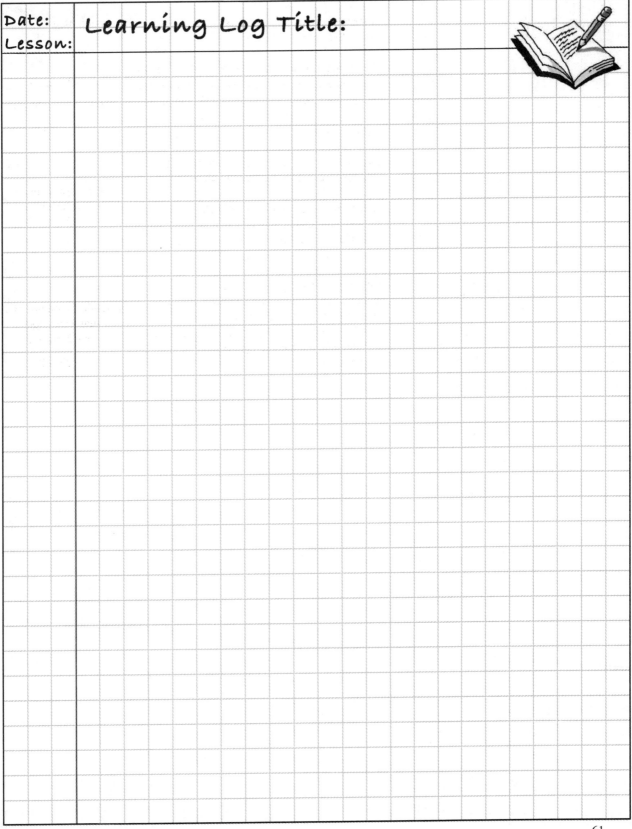

Date:	Learning Log Title:
Lesson:	

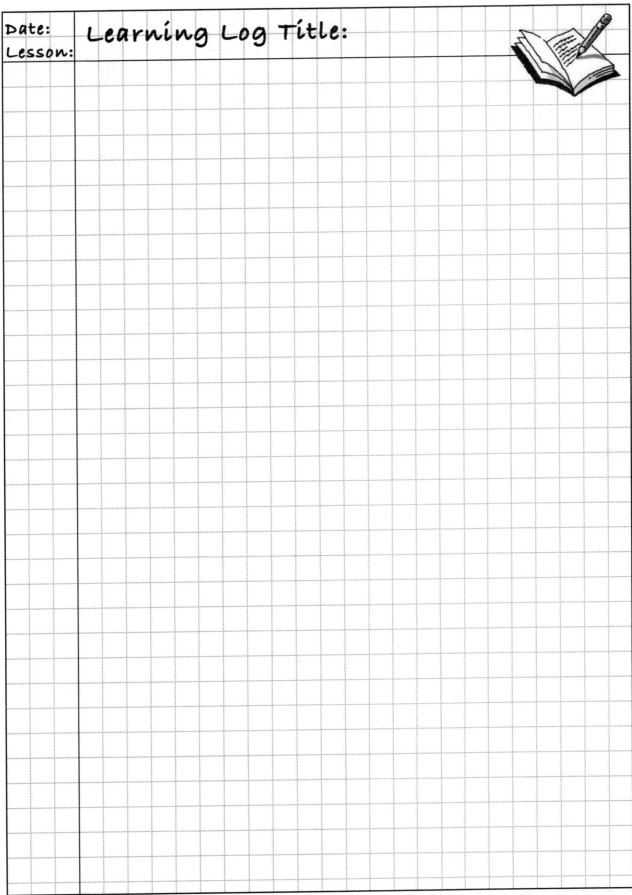

Date: Lesson:	Learning Log Title:

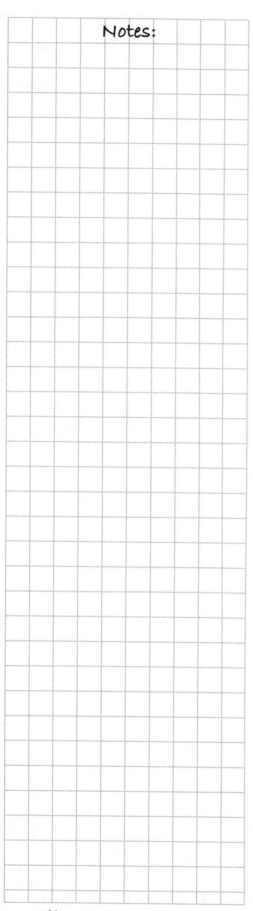

MATH NOTES

HISTOGRAMS AND STEM-AND-LEAF PLOTS

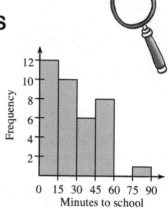

A **histogram** is similar to a bar graph in that each bar represents data in an interval of numbers. The intervals for the data are shown on the horizontal axis, and the frequency (number of pieces of data in each interval) is represented by the height of a bar above the interval.

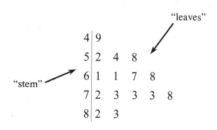

The labels on the horizontal axis represent the lower end of each interval. For example, the histogram at right shows that 10 students take at least 15 minutes but less than 30 minutes to get to school.

Histograms are used to display numeric data with an order, while bar graphs display data in categories where order generally does not matter.

A **stem-and-leaf plot** shows the same data as a histogram, but it shows the individual values from a set of data and how the values are distributed. The "stem" part of the graph represents all of the digits in a number except the last one. The "leaf" part of the graph represents the last digit of each of the numbers.

Example: Students in a math class received the following scores on their tests: 49, 52, 54, 58, 61, 61, 67, 68, 72, 73, 73, 73, 78, 82, and 83. Display the test-score data on a stem-and-leaf plot.

"leaves"

```
4 | 9
5 | 2  4  8
6 | 1  1  7  8
7 | 2  3  3  3  8
8 | 2  3
```

"stem"

QUARTILES AND INTERQUARTILE RANGE (IQR)

Quartiles are points that divide a data set into four equal parts (and thus, the use of the prefix "quar" as in "quarter"). One of these points is the median, which you learned about in Chapter 1, since it marks the middle of the data set. In addition, there are two other quartiles in the middle of the lower and upper halves: the **first quartile** and the **third quartile**.

Suppose you have this data set: 22, 43, 14, 7, 2, 32, 9, 36, and 12.

To find quartiles, the data set must be placed in order from smallest to largest. Then divide the data set into two halves by finding the median of the entire data set. Next, find the median of the lower and upper halves of the data set. (Note that if there is an odd number of data values, the median is not included in either half of the data set.) See the example below.

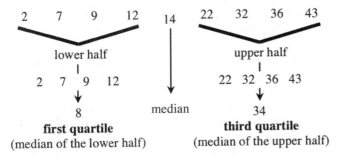

The **interquartile range** (IQR) is one way (along with range) to measure the spread of the data. Statisticians often prefer using the IQR to measure spread because it is not affected much by outliers or non-symmetrical distributions. The IQR is the range of the middle 50% of the data. It is calculated by subtracting the first quartile from the third quartile. In the above example, the IQR is 26 (34 − 8 = 26).

DESCRIBING DATA DISTRIBUTIONS

Distributions of data are typically described by considering the **center**, **shape**, **spread**, and **outliers**.

Center: The median best represents the center (or a "typical" data value) if the distribution is not symmetrical or if there are outliers. Either the mean or the median is appropriate for describing the center of symmetrical distributions with no outliers.

Shape: The shape is the overall appearance of the data when it is displayed in a histogram or stem-and-leaf plot. Is the distribution fairly symmetrical? Uniform? Single peaked? Skewed? Does it have large gaps or clusters?

Spread: Spread is a measure of the variability of the data, that is, how much scatter there is in the data. For non-symmetrical data or data with outliers, use the interquartile range (IQR) to describe the spread, since it is based on median. For symmetrical data with no outliers, either the mean absolute deviation, which is based on the mean, or the IQR are appropriate measures of spread. The range is not usually the best measure of the scatter in data, because it considers only the maximum and the minimum values and not what is occurring in between.

Outliers: An outlier is any data point that is far removed from the bulk of the rest of the data.

SCALING

When a quantity is increased or decreased by a specific proportion of the original amount, it is changed by a specific scale factor (also called a multiplier). Quantities are **scaled up** when they are increased by multiplying by a number greater than one or **scaled down** when they are decreased by multiplying by a number between (but not including) zero and one.

For example, if a music system is on sale for 25% off its original price of $500, the discount can be found by multiplying by 25%:

$$\text{discount} = 0.25(\text{original price}) = 0.25(\$500) = \$125$$

The full price (100%) minus the discount (25%) would result in the sale price, which in this case is 75% of the original. The sale price can also be found by scaling:

$$\text{sale price} = 0.75(\text{original price}) = 0.75(\$500) = \$375$$

Scaling can be used to enlarge and reduce side lengths of similar shapes, or to increase or decrease times, distances, and other related quantities.

Box Plots

A **box plot** (also known as a "box-and-whiskers" plot) displays a summary of data using the median, quartiles, and extremes of the data. The box contains "the middle half" of the data. The right segment represents the top 25% of the data, and the left segment represents the bottom 25% of the data. A box plot makes it easy to see where the data are spread out and where they are concentrated. The larger the box, the more the data are spread out.

To construct a box plot using a number line that shows the range of the data, draw vertical line segments above the median, first quartile and third quartile. Then connect the lines from the first and third quartiles to form a rectangle. Place a vertical line segment above the number line at the maximum (highest) and minimum (lowest) data values. Connect the minimum value to the first quartile and the maximum value to the third quartile using horizontal segments. The box plot is shown below for the data set 2, 7, 9, 12, 14, 22, 32, 36, and 43.

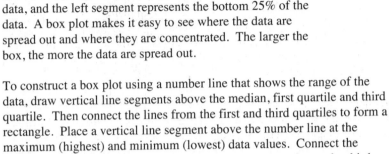

Solving Equations with Algebraic Fractions (also known as Fraction Busters)

Example: Solve $\frac{x}{3} + \frac{x}{5} = 2$ for x.

$$\frac{x}{3} + \frac{x}{5} = 2$$

This equation would be much easier to solve if it had no fractions. Therefore, the first goal is to find an equivalent equation that has no fractions.

The lowest common denominator of $\frac{x}{3}$ and $\frac{x}{5}$ is 15.

To eliminate the denominators, multiply all of the terms on both sides of the equation by the common denominator. In this example, the lowest common denominator is 15, so multiplying all of the terms (both sides) in the equation by 15 eliminates the fractions. Another approach is to multiply all of the terms in the equation by one denominator and then by the other. Either way, the result is an equivalent equation without fractions.

$$15 \cdot \left(\frac{x}{3} + \frac{x}{5}\right) = 15 \cdot 2$$

$$15 \cdot \frac{x}{3} + 15 \cdot \frac{x}{5} = 15 \cdot 2$$

$$5x + 3x = 30$$

$$8x = 30$$

In this course, the number used to eliminate the denominators is called a **Fraction Buster**. Now the equation looks like many you have seen before, and it can be solved in the usual way.

$$x = \frac{30}{8} = \frac{15}{4} = 3.75$$

Check: $\frac{3.75}{3} + \frac{3.75}{5} = 2$

$$1.25 + 0.75 = 2 \checkmark$$

Once you have found the solution, remember to check your answer.

Toolkit

PERCENT INCREASE OR DECREASE

A **percent increase** is the amount that a quantity has increased, represented as a percent of the original amount. A **percent decrease** is the amount that a quantity has decreased, written as a percent of the original amount. You can write an equation to represent a percent change that is an increase or decrease using a scale factor or multiplier:

amount of increase or decrease = (% change)(original amount)

Example 1: A loaf of bread increased in price from $0.29 to $2.89 in the past 50 years. What was the percent increase?

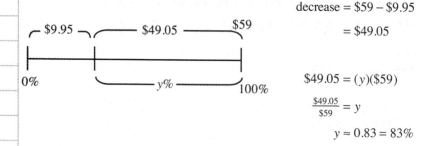

increase = $2.89 − $0.29

= $2.60

$2.60 = (x)($0.29)

$\frac{\$2.60}{\$0.29} = x$

$x \approx 8.97$ or 897%

Example 2: Calculator prices decreased from $59 to $9.95. What was the percent decrease?

decrease = $59 − $9.95

= $49.05

$49.05 = (y)($59)

$\frac{\$49.05}{\$59} = y$

$y \approx 0.83 = 83\%$

SIMPLE INTEREST

Simple interest is interest paid only on the original amount of the principal at each specified interval (such as annually or monthly). The formula to calculate simple interest is:

$I = Prt$ where P = Principal, I = Interest, r = Rate, t = Time

Example: Theresa invested $1425.00 in a savings account at her local bank. The bank pays a simple interest rate of 3.5% annually. How much money will Theresa have after 4 years?

$I = Prt$ $\Rightarrow$ $I = 1425(0.035)(4) = \$199.50$

$\Rightarrow$ $P + I = \$1425 + \$199.50 = \$1624.50$

Theresa will have $1624.50 after 4 years.

SOLVING PROPORTIONS

An equation stating that two ratios are equal is called a **proportion**. Some examples of proportions are shown at right.

$$\frac{6\,\text{mi}}{2\,\text{hr}} = \frac{9\,\text{mi}}{3\,\text{hr}}$$

$$\frac{5}{7} = \frac{50}{70}$$

When two ratios are known to be equal, setting up a proportion is one strategy for solving for an unknown part of one ratio. For example, if the ratios $\frac{9}{2}$ and $\frac{x}{16}$ are equal, setting up the proportion $\frac{x}{16} = \frac{9}{2}$ allows you to solve for x.

Strategy 1: One way to solve this proportion is by using a **Giant One** to find the equivalent ratio. In this case, since 2 times 8 is 16, so use $\frac{8}{8}$ for the Giant One.

$\frac{x}{16} = \frac{9}{2} \cdot \boxed{\frac{8}{8}}$ and $\frac{9 \cdot 8}{2 \cdot 8} = \frac{72}{16}$, which shows that $\frac{x}{16} = \frac{72}{16}$, so $x = 72$.

Strategy 2: Undoing division. Another way to solve the proportion is to think of the ratio $\frac{x}{16}$ as, "x divided by 16." To solve for x, use the inverse operation of division, which is multiplication. Multiplying both sides of the proportional equation by 16 "undoes" the division.

$$\frac{x}{16} = \frac{9}{2}$$

$$\left(\frac{16}{1}\right)\frac{x}{16} = \frac{9}{2}\left(\frac{16}{1}\right)$$

$$x = \frac{144}{2} = 72$$

Strategy 3: Use cross multiplication. This is a solving strategy for proportions that is based on the process of multiplying each side of the equation by the denominators of each ratio and setting the two sides equal. It is a shortcut for using a **Fraction Buster** (multiplying each side of the equation by the denominators).

Complete Algebraic Solution (Fraction Busters)

$$\frac{x}{16} = \frac{9}{2}$$

$$2 \cdot 16 \cdot \frac{x}{16} = \frac{9}{2} \cdot 2 \cdot 16$$

$$2 \cdot x = 9 \cdot 16$$

$$2x = 144$$

$$x = 72$$

Cross Multiplication

$$\frac{x}{16} = \frac{9}{2}$$

$$\frac{x}{16} \diagdown \frac{9}{2}$$

$$2 \cdot x = 9 \cdot 16$$

$$2x = 144$$

$$x = 72$$

Date: Lesson:	Learning Log Title:

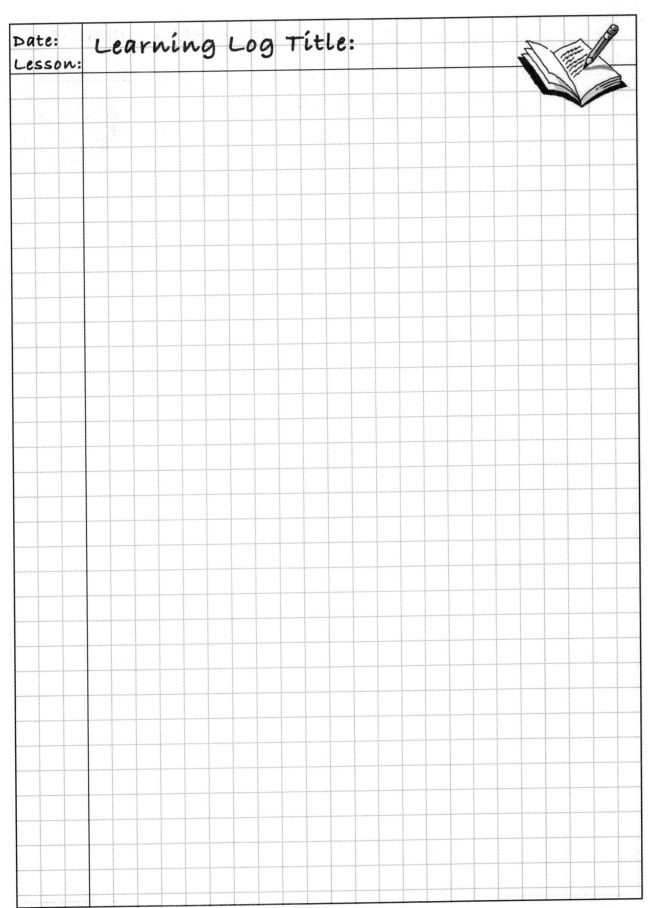

Date:

Lesson:

Learning Log Title:

Date: Lesson:	Learning Log Title:

Date: Lesson:	Learning Log Title:

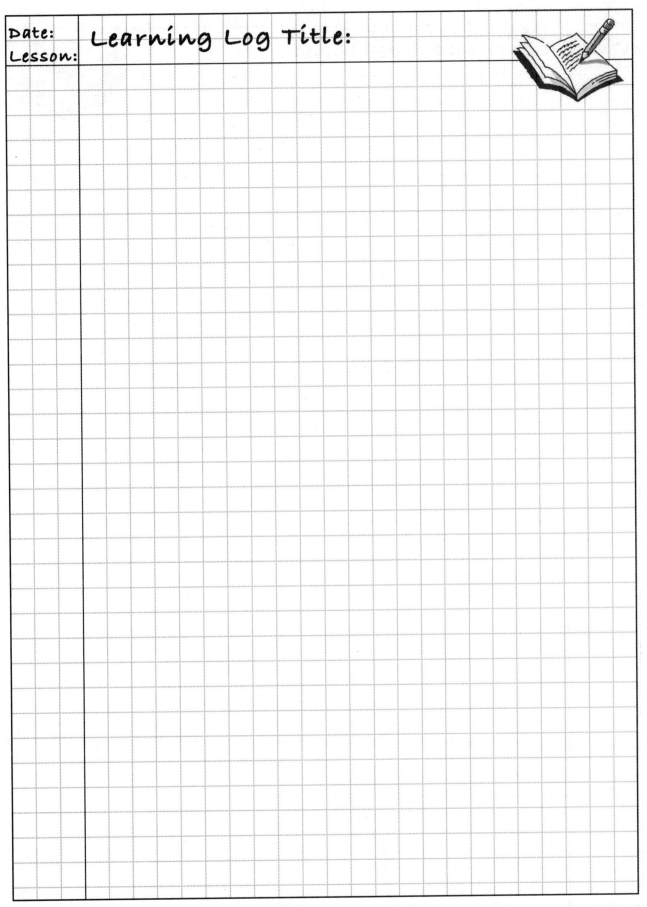

Date:	Learning Log Title:
Lesson:	

MATH NOTES

COMPARING BOX PLOTS

One way to visually represent a distribution of collected data is with a **combination histogram and box plot**. The box plot is graphed on the same *x*-axis as the histogram. See Alejandro's scores at right.

To compare two distributions, a second combination histogram and box plot is drawn *with the same scale* as the first histogram. The two combination plots can then be lined up exactly on top of each other so that differences are readily observable. Compare Alejandro's scores from above to César's scores at right.

Sometimes comparing only the two box plots is enough to be able to compare the distributions. When two box plots are drawn on the same axis, they are called **parallel box plots**. An example is shown at right.

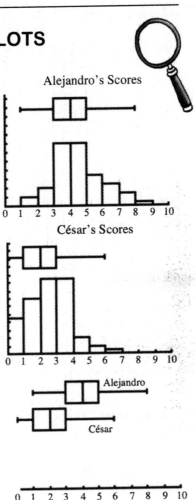

Alejandro's Scores

César's Scores

TYPES OF SAMPLES FROM A POPULATION

When taking a survey, the **population** is the group of people about whom the information is to be gathered. For example, if you wanted to conduct a survey about what foods to serve in the cafeteria, the population would be the entire student body. Since it is not usually convenient to survey the total population, different kinds of **samples** may be used.

A **representative sample** is a subgroup of the population that matches the general characteristics of the entire population. If you choose to sample 10% of the students, you would need to include an equivalent fraction of students from each grade and an equivalent ratio of male to female students as the larger population.

A **convenience sample** is a subgroup of the population where it is easy to collect data. Only sampling the students in your homeroom, for example, would be convenient, but would not necessarily accurately represent the entire school.

A **cluster sample** is a subgroup of the population that contains a common characteristic. Sampling only the eighth graders, in the above example, would be a cluster sample. Again, this sample would not necessarily represent the entire school.

A **voluntary response sample** contains only the sample of the population that chose to respond. This also would not necessarily represent the entire population.

RANDOM SAMPLES

There are many techniques for taking samples from populations. You are familiar with convenience samples, voluntary response samples, and cluster samples. However, a **random sample** is the best way to get a sample that is most representative of the population.

If you were conducting a survey, you might think it would be a good idea to pick some athletes, some band members, and some honor students to represent the school. The problem with intentionally sampling students is that it is too easy to miss an important group of students. By *randomly* picking students you would get some athletes, some band members, and some honor students. But most importantly, you would also get some students that you forgot about or did not know about, such as, the drama club students.

A random sample is representative of the whole population. Therefore, you can use random samples to make **inferences** (predictions) about characteristics of the whole population, without having to measure every single item in the population.

ANGLES

To understand the meaning of an angle, picture two rays starting at a single point called the **vertex** of the angle, as shown in the diagram at right. (A **ray** is a part of a line that starts at a point and goes on without end in one direction.)

angle

An **angle** is formed by two rays (or line segments) that have the same starting point (or **endpoint**). The **measure** of an angle is how many degrees you rotate your starting ray to get to the ray on the opposite side of an angle. One way to visualize an angle is as a measure of how "open" the gap is between the two rays.

Angles are named by their size in comparison to a right angle. That is, they are named according to whether they are less than, greater than, or equal to a right angle. An **acute angle** measures less than 90°. An **obtuse angle** measures more than 90° and less than 180°. The little box in an angle indicates that it is a **right angle**, which measures 90°). A **straight angle** measures 180° and forms a straight line.

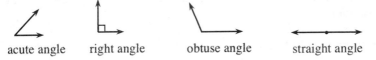

acute angle   right angle   obtuse angle   straight angle

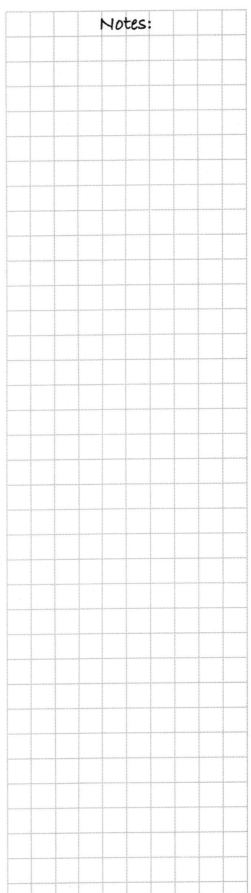

Notes:

ANGLE RELATIONSHIPS

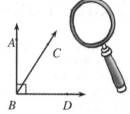

It is common to identify angles using three letters. For example, ∠*ABC* means the angle you would find by going from point *A*, to point *B*, to point *C* in the diagram at right. Point *B* is the **vertex** of the angle (where the endpoints of the two sides meet) and $\overrightarrow{BA}$ and $\overrightarrow{BC}$ are the rays that define it. A **ray** is a part of a line that has an endpoint (starting point) and extends infinitely in one direction.

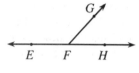

If two angles have measures that add up to 90°, they are called **complementary angles**. For example, in the diagram above right, ∠*ABC* and ∠*CBD* are complementary because together they form a right angle.

If two angles have measures that add up to 180°, they are called **supplementary angles**. For example, in the diagram at right, ∠*EFG* and ∠*GFH* are supplementary because together they form a straight angle.

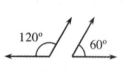

Supplementary **Complementary**

Two angles do not have to share a vertex to be complementary or supplementary. The first pair of angles at right are supplementary; the second pair of angles are complementary.

Adjacent angles are angles that have a common vertex, share a common side, and have no interior points in common. So ∠ *c* and ∠ *d* in the diagram at right are adjacent angles, as are ∠ *c* and ∠ *f*, ∠ *f* and ∠ *g*, and ∠ *g* and ∠ *d*.

Vertical angles are the two opposite (that is, non-adjacent) angles formed by two intersecting lines, such as angles ∠ *c* and ∠ *g* in the diagram above right. ∠ *c* by itself is not a vertical angle, nor is ∠ *g*, although ∠ *c* and ∠ *g* together are a pair of vertical angles. Vertical angles always have equal measure.

CIRCLE VOCABULARY

The **radius** of a circle is a line segment from its center to any point on the circle. The term is also used for the length of these segments. More than one radius are called **radii**.

A **chord** of a circle is a line segment joining any two points on a circle.

A **diameter** of a circle is a chord that goes through its center. The term is also used for the length of these chords. The length of a diameter is twice the length of a radius.

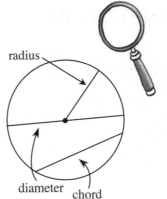

TRIANGLE INEQUALITY

For any three lengths to form a triangle, the sum of the lengths of any two sides must be greater than the length of the third side.

For example, the lengths 3 cm, 10 cm, and 11 cm will form a triangle because

$$3 + 10 > 11$$

$$3 + 11 > 10$$

$$10 + 11 > 3$$

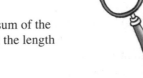

The lengths 5 m, 7 m, and 15 m will not form a triangle because $5 + 7 = 12$, and $12 \not> 15$.

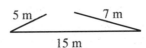

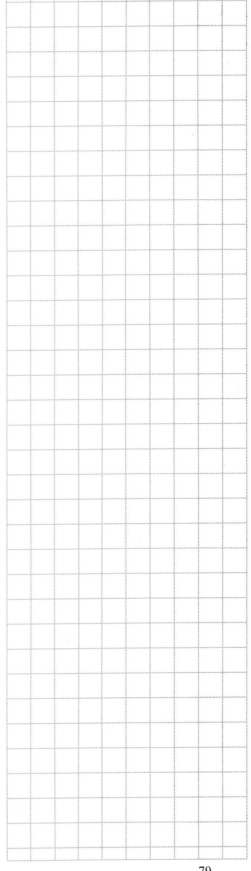

Notes:

CHAPTER 9: CIRCLES AND VOLUME

Date: Lesson:	Learning Log Title:

Date: Lesson:	Learning Log Title:

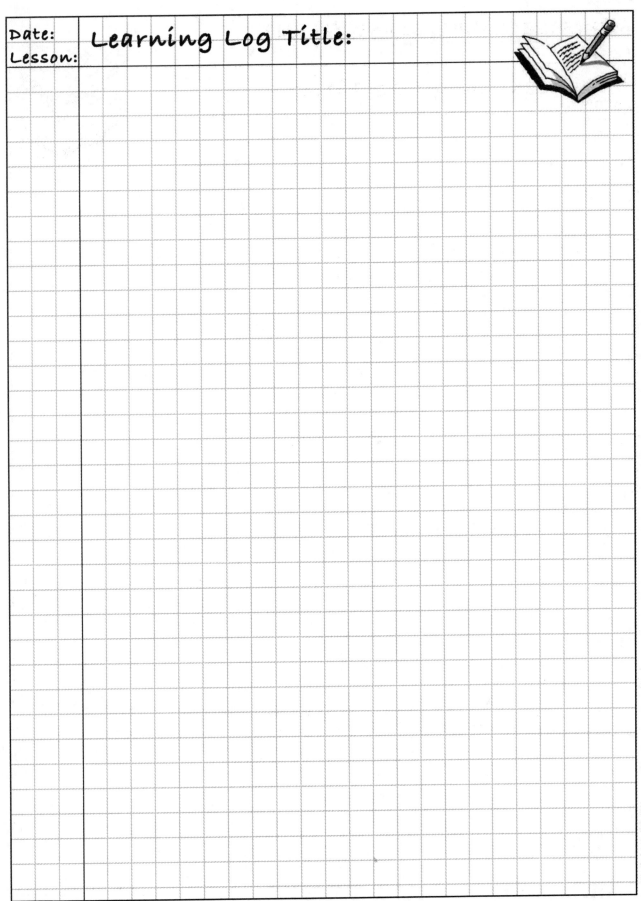

Date:
Lesson:

Learning Log Title:

Date: Lesson:	Learning Log Title:

Date: Lesson:	Learning Log Title:

MATH NOTES

CIRCUMFERENCE AND AREA OF CIRCLES

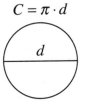

The **circumference** (C) of a circle is its perimeter, that is, the "distance around" the circle.

$$C = \pi \cdot d$$

The number π (read "pi") is the ratio of the circumference of a circle to its diameter. That is, $\pi = \frac{\text{circumference}}{\text{diameter}}$. This definition is also used as a way of computing the circumference of a circle if you know the diameter as in the formula $C = \pi d$ where C is the circumference and d is the diameter. Since the diameter is twice the radius (that is, $d = 2r$) the formula for the circumference of a circle using its radius is $C = \pi(2r)$ or $C = 2\pi \cdot r$.

The first few digits of π are 3.141592.

To find the **area** (A) of a circle when given its radius (r), square the radius and multiply by π. This formula can be written as $A = r^2 \cdot \pi$. Another way the area formula is often written is $A = \pi \cdot r^2$.

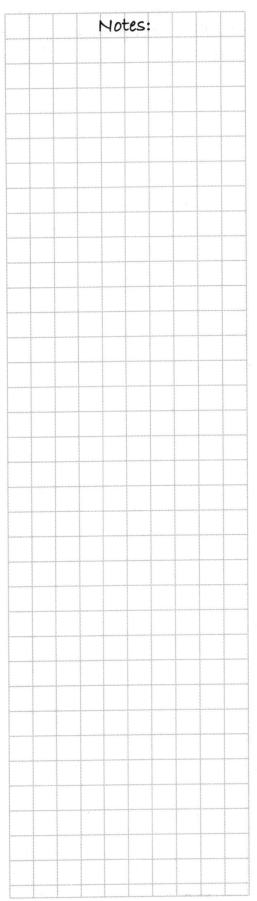

Notes:

Notes:

POLYGONS, PRISMS, AND PYRAMIDS

A **polygon** is a two-dimensional closed figure made of straight-line segments connected end to end. The segments may not cross. The point where two sides meet is called a **vertex** (plural: vertices). Polygons are named by the number of sides they have. Polygons with three through ten sides are named and illustrated below.

Triangle: Hexagon: Nonagon:

Quadrilateral: Septagon: Decagon:

Pentagon: Octagon:

Three-dimensional figures are those that have length, width, and height. If a three-dimensional figure is completely bounded by polygons and their interiors, it is a **polyhedron**. The polygons are called **faces**, and an **edge** is where two faces meet. A cube and a pyramid are each an example of a polyhedron.

face

edges

A **prism** is a special kind of polyhedron that has two congruent (same size and shape), parallel faces called **bases**. The other faces (called **lateral faces**) are parallelograms (or rectangles). No holes are permitted in the solid.

A prism is named for the shape of its base. For example:

triangular prism   pentagonal prism

A **pyramid** is a three-dimensional figure with a base that is a polygon. The lateral faces are formed by connecting each vertex of the base to a single point (the vertex of the pyramid) that is above or below the surface that contains the base.

vertex

base

MEASUREMENT IN DIFFERENT DIMENSIONS

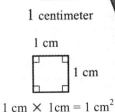

Measurements of **length** are measurements in **one dimension**. They are labeled as cm, ft, km, etc.

1 centimeter

Measurements of **area** are measurements in **two dimensions**. They are labeled as cm^2, ft^2, m^2, etc.

1 cm × 1cm = 1 cm^2

Measurements of **volume** are measurements in **three dimensions**. They are labeled as cm^3, ft^3, m^3, etc.

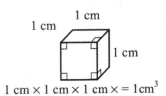

1 cm × 1 cm × 1 cm × = 1cm^3

VOLUME OF A PRISM

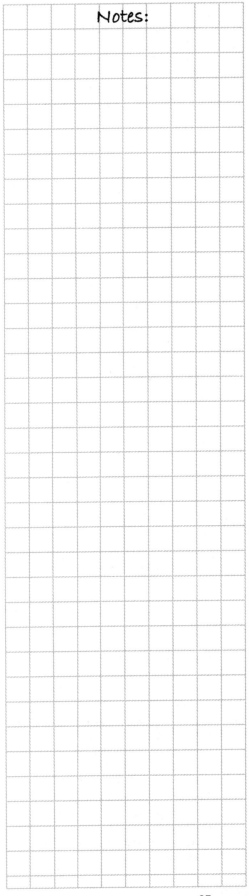

Notes:

The **volume** of a prism can be calculated by dividing the prism into layers that are each one unit high. To calculate the volume, multiply the volume of one layer by the number of layers it takes to fill the shape. Since the volume of one layer is the area of the base (B) multiplied by 1 (the height of that layer), you can use the formula below to compute the volume of a prism.

If h = height of the prism,

$$V = \text{(area of base)} \cdot \text{(height)}$$
$$V = Bh$$

Example:

Area of base = (2 in.)(3 in.) = 6 $in.^2$

(Area of base)(height) = (6 $in.^2$)(4 in.) = 24 $in.^3$

Volume = 24 $in.^3$

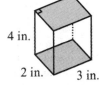

4 in.

2 in.   3 in.